HALF FULL IN MAINE

Half Full in Maine

The History and Bright Future of 10,000 Years of Optimism Down East & everywhere else

WILLEM MEINERS

Bicker Hollow

Contents

Chapter 1

Preface: Yes, Maine could have been bigger

Maine could have been bigger than it is. Not by much, but still, 900 square miles is nothing to sneeze at, equivalent to roughly the size of Rhode Island. When Maine got it offered in the year 1831, at the expense of Canada, the Mainers said no. They wanted more, thinking they'd get it by holding out, yet they ended up with less. A classic example of misplaced optimism?

Hold on to that thought.

Bangor's Stephen King once wrote a story about a bullied young girl in Lincoln County, back when he was still living in a rented doublewide in Hermon. He was in his mid twenties, insecure about writing about a cast of female characters, and reluctant to finish it. In fact, he felt so pessimistic about the early draft that he tossed it in the trash. After his wife convinced him to try again, he finally did, and then grudgingly submitted the manuscript to a publisher.

King was used to receiving rejection slips, routinely pinning them to his wall at first with a nail, later with a spike[1], once being told that "we are not interested in science fiction which deals with negative utopias. They do not sell." But this one publisher actually did say yes to the manuscript. Soon, *Carrie* was selling a million paperback copies. By early 2023, Stephen King whose genre supposedly wouldn't sell, had over 350 million books in print.

So what have we got here, the opposite? Unrealistic pessimism, one with a happy ending? It begs an interesting question. Do optimists and pessimists turn out to be wrong with equal frequency?

As we will see, the answer is a firm no. It's not even close, in Maine, or anywhere else.

But before we get to the reason why, first let's briefly go back to that missed land grab. Were Maine's decision makers realistically optimistic when they refused their extra territory in 1831, or could they have seen the pushback coming? At the heart of the issue was a big, bad thunderstorm. Lightning had hit a tree in New Brunswick during the dry late summer of 1825, which then turned into a whopper of a forest fire. It destroyed thousands of acres of timber, killed hundreds of New Brunswickers, and burned countless homes, huts and log cabins to ashes. Scared and out-of-work Canadian lumber families trekked south, into Maine, causing bedlam but insisting that there had never been an official border line drawn between England-owned Canada and the United States.

Which was true, and both London and Washington agreed that it was now time to finally settle the matter. They turned to Dutch king William I who had hosted the Treaty of Gendt negotiations after the Brits had been kicked out of the States a second time, in 1814. They didn't ask his majesty to mediate. They told him to arbitrate. Whichever boundary the king would draw, both parties would agree to. Except that when push came to shove, Maine didn't. They disagreed with king

Billy's decision, wanted more land, and figured they'd get away with it.

They would not. A decade later, ignoring Maine's objections, the U.S. and English governments agreed on a border line that gave Canada those 900 square miles. Maine had overplayed its hand, because the one thing they had underestimated was how important friendly trade between the two countries had become. By ceding the land north of St John River to Canada, each party could now utilize the waterway for their, often commonly shared, commercial purposes.

And here's a guy who would soon be very happy with that outcome. His name was Garrett Schenck from Millinocket, and he decided that he was going to build the world's largest paper mill. Garrett had an incentive that was both optimistic and realistic. By the late 1800s, America had grown in leaps and bounds, from a population of 31 million in 1860 to 63 million in 1890, and the nation was well on its way to surpassing the 100 million mark. Economic growth went through the roof. Demand for paper increased fifteen-fold during that period, as newspapers became a mass media, and weeklies and monthlies were selling like hotcakes. But also arriving was the era of Kleenex, Kotex and toilet paper, and cardboard boxes were replacing wooden crates.

And so Garrett Schenk moved to Maine, from Ohio where he was born. For centuries, paper had been predominantly made from rags, but now there were not enough rags left in the world to meet the paper demand. Wood pulp became the recipe, and therefore a papermaker had to go where the trees are. Maine is by far the U.S.'s largest forest state, with winters that in those years were long and cold enough to drag felled trees across frozen ground to rivers that would float them to the paper mill.

Garrett Schenck bought all the timberland he could get his hands on, two million acres and then some, all the way up to the St John River, unconcerned about Canadian invasions, and built two towns in the middle of nowhere, together with the largest private hydropower river dam, and, sure enough, also the world's largest paper mill. The houses in the towns were built for factory workers, and therefore he also provided schools, stores and places of entertainment, as well as railway lines for paper delivery nationwide. In Millinocket and East Millinocket, Garrett created the Great Northern Paper Company.[2]

Today, more than a century later, a whole lot less is left of Maine's once proud paper industry, for the times, they are a-changing. But in Millinocket, two schools still stand proudly, an elementary and a high school, both named for Garrett Schenck. American tongues and throats sometimes make his Amsterdam-rooted surname sound like *Skank*, therefore in 2014 a concerned grandfather of school-aged girls proposed a name change. No way, said the town council. Maine's gratitude for the man who was optimistic enough to build the world's largest paper mill is still very much alive.

* * *

This book traces the history of optimism, humanity's strongest inner drive. Optimism worldwide, nationwide, and in Maine. I decided to write this Maine companion book to my original optimism biography, *Half Full*, for two reasons. One, I live and work in Maine and, occasional neighborhood roadside attempts to convince me otherwise notwithstanding, consider it on balance one of the most optimistic places in the world. And two, *all politics is local*. It was the politician Tip O'Neill who said this, but it is just as true for readers of a book: the closer a narrative stays to what the reader perceives with their own eyes and memory, the more they recognize the main story. It was no coincidence that Tip's ancestors from Ireland first sailed to Portland in order to live in Maine for a while before moving on to Boston. Mainers stay close to themselves.

So let's get started at where and how it all began.

Optimism is like a human being. It has a past, and a date of birth. As soon as our prehistoric great-grandparents developed a much larger brain, unlike anything their own predecessors had ever possessed, ten thousand years ago, a new confidence took off. It was a growing awareness that they could impact their fate for the better. Optimism was born. Not a day too soon. After all, it's one thing for a two-legged mammal with an articulated language and a perfect set of thumbs to have the promise of a three-pound sponge bobbing inside their head. But it doesn't do much good as long as eating and taking a dump require more energy than thinking.

They had sex. We know this because they had babies. What we do not know with any degree of certainty is if hormones prompted them to multiply like, say, the Mississippi Valley wolf and the dodo did, or if instead they were primarily motivated by a frantic want for more helping hands down the road. At the end of the day, the wolf and the bird failed to make it, they became extinct. Therefore hormones alone probably weren't man's chief motivation for mating. They did need the extra hands.

For the longest time, being a member of the homo sapiens clan had been a serious challenge. Life was monotonous, dull and hopelessly uninspiring. Which was not necessarily the same thing as boring, for being constantly on the hunt for something to eat often required a whole lot more effort than they may have preferred. Between twenty and thirty thousand years ago, they left us messages about it, using finger paint on cave walls. They drew bison, deer, boars, birds, trees, plants, their entire menu. All of that had to be killed, cut or uprooted first. At least the thumbs came in handy, as did the babies once they had grown into little helpers.

And then the real hard work had yet to begin: chewing, swallowing and digesting raw food. Grandma in primeval times was one walking digestive tract, and so was grandpa. Breaking down the potpourri that kept them alive demanded all the attention their bodies could muster, and it slurped energy. Nobody grew old.

All of this changed rapidly once they learned how to cook, and that's what happened ten thousand years ago. Learning to control fire led them to bake clay and make cooking pots that didn't leak. In the pots they cooked soup. Hot water softened the meat, fish, vegetables, grains, nuts and fruits, and much of the digestion was now outsourced to the crock on the fire. In the bodies of the ancestors, the released energy was claimed by their suddenly fast expanding brain. It was the biggest deal in the entire history of humanity.

The human brain uses more fuel than any other organ. A microscope helps you to see why. The brain houses a hundred billion neurons, nerve cells. They send signals to each other at a speed of 250 miles per hour, through a network of blood vessels with a combined length of 100,000 miles[3]. All those signals and messages serve only one goal: making sure that you stay alive in the most efficient and effective manner.

Brain cells are permanently optimistic about the outcome of their effort. That's their job for life, being optimistic. Once they lose the expectation, they give up, and you die. Until then, it is one big happy festival in your brain pan. Which is quite remarkable when you stop and think about it. Because the brain owner, you, me, everyone else, does not remotely as often share their own brain cells' optimism.

Ever since ten long millennia ago fire and the cooking pot gave us the bigger brain, and with it the ability to think, ponder and plan better than any other living creature, we have surprisingly often surrendered to pessimism. Which is the more startling in light of the remarkable accomplishments our species has produced and continues to deliver in exponentially increasing ways and numbers. I use *remarkable* as an understatement because, of course, the word doesn't even remotely do the performance justice, as we will see once we open the door into the wonderland of optimism's biography.

I am a reporter by trade, straight from high school to the newsroom. The first twenty years at a newspaper in Europe, the next thirty as a storyteller and -seller in America. All this time I have marveled at the reader's want for bad news, and I'll give you an example that everyone recognizes. Each day between Europe and North America some 2,500 planes cross the Atlantic twice, there and back again. All land safely. Five thousand successful flights a day, nearly two million every year. Not a word about it in the media. Until one plane drops from the sky. That's such an exception that it hits all the front-pages. I once counted them, over twelve hundred headlines worldwide within the first twenty-four hours. Because everyone aches to know about it.

Why is that? Why do we zoom in on the one rare occasion when something goes wrong? Why do we nurture pessimism when in fact we are by design and talent consummate optimists? As the facts will show, optimism has over the course of these ten millennia become a drive so strong that it has replaced mating as humanity's number one survival tool, putting sex where it is more at home, in the realm of passion and affection. Yet we act and react persistently as if we'll be unable to keep doomsday at bay much longer.

Time for a reality check. The facts on the ground don't bear out that the apocalypse is coming. In reality, the opposite is the case, and has been all along. For not only does optimism have a past, it also has a future. A bright one, especially in Maine. Let me show you.

Chapter 2

Introduction: A golden age of pessimism?

Pessimism works overtime. It has been five minutes to midnight for so long that it must all soon go wrong, unavoidably, inescapably. Statistically it's only a matter of time, not if, but when. Nitrogen in the air. Plastic in the oceans. Too hot summers. Refugees. Face masks. Rising sea levels. Crazy hurricanes. Countries with nuclear bombs they shouldn't have. Oddball conspiracy theorists. And fake news all around, everybody and their uncle now has made-up stuff to share. We're living in the golden age of pessimism.

Except that we are not.

There are plenty of problems, troubles, challenges and dilemmas that cry out for a solution, that's crystal clear. But we are not exactly a blank slate. As a species, we have a well-documented history of awesome troubleshooting. In fact, we're so good at finding solutions to even the toughest challenges, that in this extra-large brain of ours we always find the drive to tackle the next impossible thing. It is our innate optimism, a congenital deep knowing inside informing us that one day we will get it figured out.

Except for one small detail. Everyone of us is born with a pre-wired knowledge that a single bad future incident will be inevitable. We'll drop dead. We don't know when, but one day our own life will come to a full stop. Even though we're getting better and better at pushing that episode farther down the road, sooner or later we are going to die.

But, on the flip side: everything else that the dictionary does not define as hurricanes or earthquakes is avoidable. Which is not to suggest that things never go really, badly wrong, because clearly they do, all the time. But we also know that what seems inevitable today will one day no longer be unavoidable. And if it so happens that we ourselves will no longer be here to contribute to the solution, a next generation will. For although, as the Scripture says, man's days are like grass[4], the human species at large is like weeds, here to stay indefinitely.

Remember the name of that Hungarian professor, Erno Rubik? In 1974 he invented a cube with 54 movable surfaces, each covered in one of six different colors, nine surfaces per color. Rubik's cube has 43 quintillion possible combinations, that's 43 with eighteen zeros, but only one that solves the challenge. The first time he tried, it took Rubik himself a full month to make all six sides of his cube fully green, yellow, blue, orange, red and white, respectively. Eight years later, the first world championship "Solving Rubik's Cube" was held. The winner did it within 23 seconds[5].

Or there's the example of Lego, the Danish toy manufacturer. When in 1949 they switched to making little plastic building blocks, there was an idea behind it. Until then, almost no children's toys were mutually compatible. Parents bought for their kids a doll, a crib, a dollhouse, a fire engine or a train, all produced differently, from different materials, typically made by different manufacturers. With the plastic Lego blocks, children could suddenly build everything themselves, houses, cars, animals, T-rex, rockets, the possibilities are endless. Why? Because just six blocks alone, each with eight studs, allow for 915 million different combinations[6]. So imagine what you can do with 15 million blocks. With that many, Lego built an entire amusement park in Billund, Denmark.

Numbers with more than a few zeros can make people dizzy, but those same people have once played with Lego, or with the cube. Regardless of how likely or not it is that we will one day come up with this or that solution, the illustration of simple toys confirms what the brain has known for a long time: complicated things are doable, challenges will one day be mastered.

The world today is better than at any other time in history. List as many burning issues as you can come up with, and they're all true and pressing, yet life today is better, safer, healthier, more comfortable and more entertaining for the vast majority of people on Earth than ever before. That's no coincidence, it took ten thousand years of hard work, using this one constant drive, the one motivation that keeps armageddon away, optimism. As a rule, the optimist does not accept that anything is forever unsolvable. Each human being accepts defeats and setbacks, but only temporarily. And if our own deadline happens to catch up with us first, there's always someone else that will finish the job.

Which is one reason why we are now all walking around with a small six by three-inch tablet, ultra thin, available in all colors of the rainbow, that we have given the old-fashioned name "telephone". In fact, it is in essence a Swiss invention from the year 1890[7], when that country gave its soldiers a pocket knife that also contained a screwdriver, an awl, a can opener and a key to open and repair their rifles with.

Our handheld is a radio, a TV, a camera, a computer, a calculator, a means of payment, a flashlight, a battery meter, a dictionary, a video and audio recorder, a text and email sender and receiver, a library, a bookcase, a shopping center, a type-writer, a GPS, a weather forecaster, a translator mastering 133 languages, a photo album, a telephone, a clock, a stopwatch, a magnifying glass, a mirror, an alarm clock and three million other applications that we can load for free or for pennies from the apps store.

Thirty years ago none of this existed. Back then there were no doctor consultations via your laptop, electric cars that re-charge by driving on a highway paved with solar panels, robots in nursing homes that roll up to check whether grandpa has taken his pills and that warn the nurse when grandma has a fever, takeout meals that are drone-delivered on your doorstep, or a vaccination against skin cancer. It's all here now, and each of these examples is just in its early stages. No one yet knows what will soon be possible with artificial intelligence, crypto payments, robots, or self-driving traffic.

All we do know is that in less than no time we're going to think it's all standard. Like anything else that would have astonished us ten, fifty, a hundred, much less a thousand years ago.

***

So we're going to explore ten millennia of optimism history together. Feel free to hold me accountable for the sightseeing as I navigate us from one point of interest to the next. But while I will do the narrating, other people and events will do most of the talking. They include Nelson Mandela, a movie star, a skinny general in Spain's parliament who would not accept a military coup d'état, and Newcastle's Frances Per-kins, another Mainer who shaped America. All of them brave optimists who refused to get discouraged. You will hear from the dictionary editor who knows all seven hundred thousand words of the English language by heart but finds his optimism challenged when he hits a wordless wall at home. There's lunch with a tormented defense secretary Robert McNamara who avoided a nuclear war but lost a non-nuclear one and who spent a lifetime not understanding what went wrong. Central character at that lunch: Mount Desert Island resident Roswell Gilpatric, a man who once made all the difference. And then there's Nora Brown, the bestselling author who gets it, who does understand what makes women tick.

We'll be looking at the biology and the genetics of optimism, at the unshakable optimism of love and marriage, at the strongly increased power of women everywhere, at children's fascinations for bad guys, and at how nations and cultures compare. We'll stop in Portugal, Greece, ancient Rome, and Spain. We'll compare America with the Dutch, and the Brits with Germany and France. Optimism brings us to Iceland, China, Russia, and India, and we are making excursions to Africa, Turkey and Japan. We are checking in with classical doomsayers Thomas Hobbes and Robert Malthus, and also with their more sunny opposite numbers Jean-Jacques Rousseau and little miss Pollyanna.

And then there are the risk takers, the adventurers. Not the gamblers, but mavericks such as Annie who was the first to survive dropping down Niagara Falls, or blind Joe who became the world's first hacker, Jeff who built the largest store in the world, and Isabella who, as a queen, demanded something real to reign over. Abbot Nollet who electrocuted his monks and in so doing laid the foundation for the telegraph, and Harpa, the cow that ran away from the butcher and inspired an entire nation. There's carpenter John who saved countless sailors from drowning, and young Tilly, the girl who did the same for a hundred beach tourists.

We live in a world of opposites, therefore where there's optimism, there is also pessimism. We'll look at it when we zoom in on the history of conspiracy theorists, on Donald Trump's voters and on my neighbors in rural Maine for whom change is happening too fast. But pessimism doesn't balance out optimism, much less halts it. When optimism clashes, as it often does, it is with realism.

Wishing, not knowing for certain, yet firmly believing despite earlier adversity: that's optimism. Samuel Johnson, the 18th-century essayist, once summarized this with, "Hope triumphs over experience." Dreaming, also wishing and hoping, yet sensing that this is as far as we can go today: that's realism. Recognizing the difference has prevented many a disaster in history. Not recognizing it has caused accidents and calamities.

I will be your navigator in this chronicle, because navigating is something I have done before, for real, years ago when I attempted to cross the Andes mountain range in a small helicopter. Flying, like space travel, is one of history's more spectacular accomplishments of optimism because it brazenly defies the laws of physics. In all ten thousand years of people with larger-than-before brains, they have been staring with envy at birds and butterflies. All this time they have wished to be capable of flying, but only since 1903 have they figured out how to do it. Through costly trial and error. Today, aircraft accidents are an exception, but only because we have learned from mistakes, failures and unknowns. For many years, flying was hazardous, downright dangerous, and often courting death.

A hundred years after Orville and Wilbur Wright succeeded, I took flying lessons and bought a small helicopter, a four-seater. I criss-crossed the continent, together with Norwegian, Dutch, American, English and German pilots, admiring the united beauty of America's fifty states from an altitude of a thousand feet. Seeing the world from a helicopter is intoxicating, addictive, and I developed an urge to be the first to cover a uniquely long distance[8]. Unique, as in: flying south from the tiny town of Barrow[9] at the very top of Alaska to Ushuaia at the very bottom of Argentina, tracking the full length of the Pacific shoreline before turning towards the Atlantic and following its coastline northbound until I got home again. No one had done it before, not in a helicopter, and certainly not in such a small one.

I felt optimistic about pulling it off. Mainly because an expedition like that is not one long trek, but a hundred short ones, each lasting a few hours until the fuel runs out and it is time to land and refill. Every next decision whether or not to take off to an unknown destination, over unknown terrain, is preceded by a meeting between optimism and realism, each time. Here and there in this book I share a hairy moment or two, using them as a coat rack so to speak, for what has motivated and moved others who over the course of ten millennia have sought to check off yet another "not been done before".

***

There is a species of trees known as the quaking aspen. They grow in my backyard, the woodland edge of a dense forest that stretches north a thousand miles from Maine's Penobscot River deep into Canada. The tree name refers to the sound the leaves make as the wind stirs them. They vibrate and sing. A colony of aspens of that species is interconnected underground. All of its trees have originated from one and the same tree seed, which continues to cause new aspens to grow. They all share one root system, and although individual trees eventually die and fall over, the root system remains alive for hundreds, sometimes thousands of years.

The quaking aspen is a metaphor. Is history caused by something similar, does it consist of moments and events and decisions that flow from one another, that are all interconnected by one and the same root incident, and therefore are inevitable? Here's an example. Nine days after World War I broke out in 1914, President Wilson's wife died in the White House. At a time when events in Europe demanded his full attention, the man was inconsolable. But not for long, because a few months later he met the rosy-cheeked widow of a Washington jeweler, who had just returned from an extensive canoe vacation in Maine[10]. She was sixteen years younger and a flirt, he was the son of a pastor. They got married very quickly.

When Edith Wilson talked to the president, she did so with a passion. She told him that he was the messiah the world needed right now, a leader, a people's shepherd. It went over well, for Woodrow Wilson had always felt he had a missionary's urge. In each town where he lived, he had joined the church choir, and whenever the singing began, it would choke him up[11]. The effect of Edith's words was that, immediately after the war ended, the president traveled to Europe, for six long months, to be the peacemaker there. She joined him, but he left his cabinet ministers and most of his assistants at home.

Wilson was no good as a negotiator. He was so obstinate, others said arrogant and pompous, that the Versailles Treaty which he concocted ended up having no practical value. If he had let the experts and the competents do their job, much better workable agreements would likely have been reached, and Europe would not within two decades uncontrolledly have slipped into a second war. After having caught the Spanish flu and returned from Paris, Wilson suffered a debilitating stroke. Edith kept him shielded and locked inside their bedroom and then made a series of presidential decisions on his behalf until the end of his term.

Events behaving like an aspen colony[12], one naturally leading to the next. What began with the death of the first Mrs. Wilson just as World War I started, ended with the outbreak of World War II. Inevitably?

It seems like a tempting conclusion. But as we will see, there's a lot more nuance to history, with crossroads, and with options at every turn, each nuance and each crossroads an opportunity to impact fate. Let's take a look.

Chapter 3

Mandela, the cardinal, the jumper, and the bathroom

Optimism, realism, and wishful thinking

On the seventh floor, Nelson Mandela stepped into the elevator. We were both staying at the same hotel in Kyoto. He was taller than I had imagined, his shoulders slightly bent, but his face was like everyone knew it, friendly, smiling, short cropped almost-grey hair. He wished me a good morning. On the fourth floor, the elevator door opened again and a young woman walked in. She was wearing the hotel reception uniform, and she addressed him, nervously. "Mr. Mandela, management asks if you would please sign the VIP guestbook."

He didn't hesitate. "Of course. If the VIPs don't mind."

It is my favorite anecdote from the three days I spent around him. It was April 22, 1991, he was not yet chair of his political party, ANC, and it would be another three years before he would be elected president of South Africa. He had

17

only fourteen months earlier been released from prison after having been locked up for more than a quarter of a century for his belief that black and white should have equal rights. While we were in that elevator, Apartheid was still a fact. But not in Nelson Mandela's head. There, it was already abolished. He was going to win this.

We had both been invited to one of the conferences hosted by the International Press Institute during my years as a member, in cities such as Kyoto, Istanbul, Berlin and Bordeaux. This sometimes yielded surprising encounters. I shook the fist of Manuel Gutierrez Mellado, a short, slender man of 76, officially a marquis, but the world knew him better from when rebel soldiers attempted a coup in Madrid. They occupied the Spanish parliament in front of live TV cameras. Guttierrez was both a general and Spain's defense minister, he rose from behind his desk and scolded the insurgents, demanding their surrender. They tried to push him over, but he didn't flinch. I understood why as soon as he shook my hand. An iron fist. The Madrid coup in 1981 failed.

The following year I got a hug from singer and actress Melina Mercouri, then 69. On the day Greek colonels in her country forcibly overturned democracy, April 21, 1967, she was staying on Broadway in New York. Mercouri, nominated for an Oscar for her role in the film *Never on Sunday*, started an international resistance movement without delay. The colonels responded by stripping her of her passport and her citizenship. She was barred from ever coming home. Her response, "I was born a Greek and will die a Greek. Those bastards were born fascists and they will die fascists." She was right. Melina Mercouri not only died as a Greek, but also as the longest-serving minister of arts and culture in Greek history. In 1994, she received a state funeral in Athens.

Sometimes the meeting location was quite informal. With Cardinal Jaime Sin of Manila, aged sixty and dressed in a fluttering black and purple cassock, I walked side by side to the men's room. He pointed his chin at the ladies' door and indicated that he liked women. The cardinal who had introduced himself with, "My name is Sin; without sin there is no Savior," had recently played a key role in the fall of Ferdinand and Imelda Marcos's regime by leading the way in street protests and blocking army tanks. He disappeared into a stall, left the door open, fumbled with his cassock, urinated, then boomed a loud fart. He didn't give a damn.

In Kyoto, Nelson Mandela was the guest of honor. Of the four chairs on the podium, for that morning's speakers, Mandela took the one closest to the wings. His turn to say something was to come once Japan's crown prince had finished speaking. But that took a while, and Mandela decided that he, too, had to make a sanitary stop. So he got up in front of a packed hall, disappeared between the wings, did what he had to do and returned right on time. Unembarrassed, just doing as he pleased, a man who, after 27 years behind bars, had lost any and all concern for what others might expect of him.

The cardinal, the skinny general with his fist of steel, the actress, and the released prisoner who almost single-handedly put an end to Apartheid. Total optimists.

***

But each also significantly older than most other people. Which invites the question: who is more optimistic, a young woman or an older man? A twenty-five-year-old guy or an elderly lady? No one would react with disbelief if you'd say that younger people are still filled with hope and expectation, and that older people have seen enough to have become cynical. So: the younger, the more optimistic?

On the other hand, younger people feel more scrutinized and judged than their elders. Their looks are still important to them, at this stage they are more aware of their posture and appearance. They spend longer in front of the mirror, and they are not easily satisfied with what they see.

There's a man who put this phenomenon to the test. Gil Zamora worked for the FBI and for the San Jose, California police department for sixteen years, as a forensic sketch artist. Crime witnesses would tell him what the suspect looked like, and Gil then drew as close a sketch as possible. When he started out on his own, he rented an abandoned office space, and filled it with only a work table, a stool for himself and an easy chair for a guest. Between the two seats he hung a curtain. When the guest entered, he sat with his back to her. He and she could not see each other.

Gil asked her to describe her own face, eyes, hair, chin, forehead, mouth, the shape of her nose. He sketched as she spoke, just as he had done at the FBI and the police. When he had heard enough, he sent her away, and in her place next came someone else who, at his request, had spent some time with her earlier that day. Gil Zamora asked him or her the same questions, not about themselves, but about the woman who had been his earlier guest. Based on their descriptions he made another sketch.

Without exception, the difference between the two drawings was one of night and day. A person's own view of themselves was much more negative than another's view. When Gil then invited the first woman back and showed her the two sketches, she invariably became quiet, and emotional. These were women averaging between thirty and forty years of age. They had every reason to be more optimistic about their appearance than in fact they were[13].

Psychologists, sociologists, historians, physiologists, economists, neurobiologists, anthropologists, neuroanatomists - they all have over the course of the previous century conducted an exhaustive research into what drives people to optimism. The century gave them plenty of motive. With two world wars, it was the most violent in history. At the same time it was also by far the most successful, with spectacular leaps forward in combating infant mortality, poverty, disease, hunger, income inequality and educational disadvantages. Let alone the unprecedented increase in comfort, mobility and access to information. How could an era that had left so many people pessimistic have such a Janus face? How could it, in spite of everything horribly bad, have inspired so many more people to feeling optimistic?

The result of all that sleuthing led to conclusions that were sometimes surprising, and sometimes completely obvious. One: everybody possesses an innate sense of optimism and expresses it every day, as we'll see in the next chapter. Two: the degree of our optimism grows as we age - which was the correct answer: the older, the more optimistic.[14] For three perfectly understandable reasons. Optimism grows as we become better at what we do at work or as parents of children. It grows as we become more self-sufficient, because that's when our awareness of independence increases, and the more independent, the happier. And the third factor is our connection with others. The better our social contacts, the more optimistic we tend to be.

A young woman in her twenties may feel perfectly well connected to her friends and colleagues through her social contacts. A man in his thirties may feel that he is being a really good dad to his kid. But despite this, they may both come to the conclusion that they still feel dependent on the approval of their parents or their employer, or on the social rules and expectations around where they live. This wears off, or if you will: they grow out of it, over time. As they get older, they feel more and more confident, which determines the increase in their optimism.

All of these research findings had an interesting footnote. The threshold for whether or not you feel like an optimist also has a hereditary factor. Those who have a predominantly optimistic parent or grandparent behave more sunny themselves - by a quarter. One of the studies showing this involved five hundred twins.[15] Half had grown up together in the same family. The other half consisted of twins who had as babies both been adopted, but each by a different set of parents. The first group underwent the same experiences throughout their childhood, had the same upbringing under the same roof. The others had grown up completely different, with dissimilar exposures, experiences and values. But no matter how different their history was, they shared one quarter of the same degree of optimism.

Economist and Nobel laureate Daniel Kahneman, who made a study of the behavior of stock traders on Wall Street, found so much optimism there that for a moment he thought he was dealing with as much as a hundred percent heredity. They all behave like start-ups, he said, even though "the chances that a small business will survive for five years in the United States are about 35 percent," one in three.[16] But none of the start-ups believe that this probability applies to them. The same, he concluded, is true on Wall Street. No stockbroker thinks of themselves as taking too much investment risk. "Because they misread the risks, optimistic entrepreneurs believe they are prudent even when they are not." Kahneman did not rule out that it was due to a hundred percent innate, and therefore incorrigible, trait. He was only a quarter right. Investors are also average people.

***

I myself am an optimist, by and large. I'll give you as an example that helicopter, a Robinson-44, a small aircraft with four seats. Together with a German pilot and an Icelandic photographer, on July 20, 2007, I flew along the Brazilian coast on our way to Rio de Janeiro, northbound.[17] Earlier that day we had landed on the white sand of what the Brazilians call *Praia Desertinho*, Portuguese for what is indeed a completely deserted beach. It is locked in by tall, overgrown cliffs, perfectly inaccessible to all means of transportation including your feet, except by boat. Or by helicopter. Brazil has one of the longest coastlines in the world, five thousand miles. This idyllic beach is one of the gems along that coast. For a moment it felt like I was getting a glimpse of what paradise must have looked like.

By the time the helicopter approached Rio after that beach visit, it had gotten dark. It was winter below the equator; the sun set around half past five. The evening was cloudless, there was no wind to speak of, and the GPS indicated that we were flying at an altitude of fifteen hundred feet above the water and that the mountains along the coast were safely to our left. Air traffic control knew we were coming, we had filed a flight plan, and they saw us on their radar.

When the mountain range interrupted itself and the city behind it suddenly came into clear view, we were instructed to make the left turn and enter into a final descent to Santos Dumont Airport. With the lights of the city in the background, I saw Rio's famous Sugarloaf Mountain looming ahead of us. It had two peaks, I noticed, one tall and the other much lower. Right in between, in the distance, was the runway. It was yet another pretty sight, coming on the heels of earlier having marveled at that beautiful beach, now this big city, the silhouette of Sugar Loaf Mountain, and beyond it the runway illuminated by the flashes of what in aviation lingo are known as rabbit lights. We flew straight towards them.

Suddenly it came at us at a speed of more than a hundred miles per hour. An overhead cable, and then another one. Pilot Stephan and I both knew from our early weeks of flight training what that meant. Flying into overhead wires is cause number one of helicopter accidents because in the air they are barely discernible, as every student pilot is reminded of with dramatic video footage. Between the two peaks of its popular mountain, Rio runs cable cars. In a split second, Stephan pulled the cyclic aft toward him, while his left hand simultaneously yanked the collective up. These two inputs together pushed the nose of the helicopter upward, with added engine power, causing the aircraft to slow down and to climb sharply. I watched the cables pass below our skids in a flash. Had we detected them three seconds later, we would have crashed.

We had no choice but to quickly return to business as usual, because we were flying, and there was still an airport approach to be finalized and a landing to be made. Within minutes, we were safely on the ground. The next morning, after a good night's sleep on the Copacabana and a hearty breakfast in a hotel guarded by men with machine guns, it was only in daylight that we really saw what we had escaped. The parked helicopter looked from the airport helipad straight at the two mountain peaks in the distance. They had sixteen cables between them.

It is funny how the mind deals with such situations. They do not negatively affect your optimism. If anything, they reinforce it. Everyone who is saved by the bell, who has just beaten odds, feels a tad more invincible. Also, all is well that ends well. It was unlikely that we would make a similar mistake again. This was day 78 of that expedition that took us from Alaska to Argentina and back, and, rightly or wrongly, by now we felt fairly seasoned. We had reached Ushuaia on July 13, a week before Rio. Since then we had been tracking the Atlantic coast back up north. I estimated that we still had about three weeks of flying ahead of us until we'd be back home in Maryland. By then we would have covered forty thousand miles.

All that in the name of doing something that no one else had done before, it was all about the challenge. That, and to raise awareness for children's hospitals in some twenty countries, to encourage people to send get-well-soon cards to sick children. And before you think: how nice - there are much nicer people in the world. In Providence, Rhode Island hundreds, sometimes a few thousand, of people have for years been blinking their flashlights, headlamps and phones every evening at 8:30 p.m. to bid the little patients in a children's hospital good night.

Anyway, we had encountered many obstacles along the way, nothing was easy, but every pitfall had been avoided. It would be unlikely for this pattern to change in the remaining three weeks. All sorts of things can go wrong as soon as you defy gravity, but pilots are well trained and we had prepared thoroughly for this project. Now we had goofed, by not paying enough attention while approaching Rio, briefly distracted by the day's views, but it was history, it was behind us. I had no doubts about the all is well that ends well part.

***

Here's a similar example, different angle, different time. Ever heard of Annie Edson? Frankly, you should have. On October 24, 1901, she decided to step into an oak barrel, also for the purpose of setting a record. It was her birthday, she turned 63 that day, and she wanted to be the first human to dive over the edge of Niagara Falls and arrive at the bottom in one piece. On the inside of the barrel she had attached two handles to hold onto. A mattress served as padding for protection. Everyone who heard about it declared her crazy, but of course people came nonetheless flocking to the waterfall, by the thousands, to watch the spectacle. Annie herself was optimistic about the outcome, especially after she had performed a test dive on the American side of the Niagara River. She had locked her pet cat inside the barrel and pushed it over the edge. Cat and barrel both survived.

Ms. Daredevil had been a teacher, so she knew where to find information about weather forecasting, especially rain and wind, and she measured the effect of weight on speed. Therefore she had a 200-pound anvil attached to the bottom of the 160-pound barrel. That way she'd be down faster, feet first.

Annie Edson was a descendant of Philip de Lannooij, an early Dutch emigrant to America. De Lannooij was a name that hardly anyone across the ocean could pronounce properly so, once he had arrived overseas, Phil re-spelled it Delano. Annie's grandfather on her dad's side came from the Delano family. It made her a remote cousin of President Ulysses Grant and a great-aunt of future President Franklin Roosevelt. She was unaware of this, and either way, it didn't help her. Annie Edson was penniless.

This was the reason she wanted to set the record. She hoped to make money from it, as an old-age security. She had hired a manager who sent out a few press releases here and there. Those said that Annie's father was a miller who died when she was twelve, that she got married and had a son, and that the baby had died in the crib, soon followed by the death of Annie's husband. It was a tragic story, with a few blank spaces, because although she was formally 63 on the day of her record attempt, she could also have been 64. No one knew for sure, because Annie Edson would occasionally fib about her age.

U.S. and Canadian local authorities tried to prohibit her from taking the fall. To which she responded by threatening to commit suicide in public. The authorities gave in, but warned the manager that if his client did not survive, he would be arrested for manslaughter.

She did survive. Helpers had closed the lid over her head. Through a hole they had injected air into the barrel with a bicycle pump, and she herself had closed the hole with a plug.

Annie floated for fifteen minutes on the Niagara's current towards the Horseshoe Falls, plunged 158 feet down, and then waited without injury until another team of helpers pulled her ashore. At that point things almost went south after all; the saw they used for opening the barrel gashed her cheek, but Annie wasn't the type to fret over a face cut.

And that's where the success story ended. Because while Annie Edson went to use a bathroom in a nearby hotel, the manager took off with the barrel, along with a young lady friend who from then on pretended to be Annie. The two scammers went from one carnival to the next, collecting the money that Annie had hoped to spend on getting old carefree. Stuntwoman Annie Edson remained as broke as she already was and died twenty years of poverty later, still penniless.

***

She was neither stupid nor suicidal. "This has nothing to do with a suicide attempt as far as I'm concerned," she said in an interview a week before she stepped into the barrel. "I have complete confidence that I'm going to survive the fall unscathed."[18] It was more a matter of probability, a weighing of risks. Her life had been marked by the sudden deaths of father, husband and son. It could all be over just like that. Probability calculations vary between best and worst case scenarios. Annie's best outcome was an injury-free fall followed by wealth. The worst was that she would crash and die. The latter didn't matter much to her, sudden death was something she was used to, and she had no kin to worry about.

As far as survival was concerned, she was right, which was remarkable enough because the plunge had been tried for years by earlier daredevils. They had all perished, whereas Annie walked away with a 3-inch scratch. She was, however, wrong about her wealth expectation. Do it one more time, then? No way: "I would sooner walk up to the mouth of a cannon, know-ing it was going to blow me to pieces than make another trip over the fall," she said afterwards.[19] She was an optimist and the classic example of a risk taker who tries something no one has successfully done before. Michelle Wucker, an economist who advises governments on how to calculate risk, summed up Annie Edson with the title of the book in which she portrays the Niagara heroine as an example, "You are what you risk."[20]

But was Annie also a realist? And what about me? Above, I described myself an optimist, "by and large". I added the ca-veat because in Salamanca when visiting my daughter I prefer not to cross that big square at the Plaza Mayor. I rather walk around it, staying closer to the buildings. Also, after surviving two head-on collisions in my late teens, I don't much care for being my own driver, I'm better as a co-pilot. And in a movie theater or the ballpark, I prefer an aisle seat, ideally in the back row. You feel easily trapped, the therapist said to me. You want emergency exits, you want to be able to make your own choice between fight and flight. True, but it is unreasonable when in reality there's nothing that poses a threat. Except a vague feel-ing we all recognize, which says: you never know, it could go wrong, and then you can't escape. And that's an expression of pessimism.

None of which has anything to do with realism. Daniel Kah-neman's investors on Wall Street were lousy realists, for they demonstrably kept misjudging their risks. On the other hand, Annie Edson correctly assessed that she could go down with the waterfall without incident. This, despite the fatal results of all the attempts before her, was ultimately realistic. Getting rich, in theory, was a much lesser risk, and yet that's where things went wrong.

As for me, I reasonably estimated that I would get home safely with my crew mates, even though we still had the stretch across what was popularly known as Colombia's *Kidnap Alley* ahead of us. Didn't bother the optimist in me. I was a fan of smart-ass Samuel Johnson's and his claim that "hope triumphs over experience." That's because the sunny expectation of what tomorrow will bring often outweighs yesterday's *oops*.

***

Nelson Mandela stayed around for a while that week in Japan. He wanted to see the temples of Kyoto since he had read about them in prison. I stood side by side with him again as the guide explained the stones in the temple garden, and the raked sand. Nothing about him betrayed how the man had been belittled, humiliated and hurt for years. He stood proud and unbroken, a seventy-two-year-old with a brilliant future. A rock star. Japanese teenage girls, on a school trip to learn about the temple, nudged each other, with eyes like saucers, chattering like young blackbirds. At home just last night, they had seen him on television.

Nothing instills feel-good better than being in the proximity of a true optimist.

Chapter 4

Widespread optimism that you barely notice

The optimism of trusting blindly

An optimist is someone who trusts in a positive result. Sometimes based on readily available facts, but much more often blindly. Because blindly also has its own set of facts, usually based on that combination of probability and an assessment of worst case scenarios. Everyone trusts blindly, day in and day out. You bite into something from a plastic bag and trust that it's really a slice of bread. You fill your glass from a half-gallon container that a total stranger has placed in the refrigerated section of a supermarket, and believe without question what it says: milk. You put the pharmacist's pills in your mouth, you drive through a green light trusting it to be red on the side street, you let your child walk to the schoolbus stop and drive yourself to work unconcerned, and you assume that because the hotel room towels smell clean they are in fact clean. You go to sleep expecting to wake up the next morning.

That's optimism based on an intuitive probability calcula-tion. For while some people do go postal and it's therefore conceivable that sometime, somewhere, some ticked-off bak-ery employee has left a razor blade inside a loaf of bread, or that there's a tiny chance a shipment of milk might somehow contain dissolved strychnine, and that occasionally a motorist is texting while driving and therefore fails to see their red traffic light, much more often things do go right. Very much more often. In 2020, 327 million Americans ate bread every day, sixty loaves that year per capita, a total of nearly twenty billion loaves sold. No one reported finding anything sharp. It did happen in pizza dough, though - a few miles from where I live in Maine, a laid-off employee hid razor blades in ready made dough that year. He got caught.[21]

People are constantly doing calculations in their heads. Almost all planes land safely. Almost every mile you travel during your lifetime is obstacle-free. Most houses don't burn down. The man or woman in uniform on the street is really a police officer and not a terrorist. Lightning strikes somewhere else, not you. The number of infant deaths is not expressed in percentages, but in one promille.[22] And you have of course every reason to expect that you, like some eight billion others, will wake up tomorrow morning: your odds of not waking up are an average 1 in 170,000. That is equivalent to one unlucky person in four packed arenas, and the younger you are, the more your odds improve. Armed with that knowledge, some-times no more than a legitimate but vague suspicion, a person assesses their own chances that things will turn out okay to-day based on a well-founded optimism.

This comes as a surprise to the pessimist. All they know is that the Oxford dictionary has it right: "Pessimism - expect-ing bad things to happen or something not to be successful." That's us to a T, pessimists say about themselves. I once of-fered someone a helicopter ride during her lunch break. Among aviators, those flights are known as *100-dollar hamburgers*. It's when you fly to another airport where there's a restaurant, you eat something, and then you fly back. The depreciation on your aircraft, along with the cost of fuel, means that your lunch will easily set you back a hundred bucks per passenger.

Danielle enjoyed her very first helicopter flight. She had brought an expensive pair of sunglasses, and she put them on when she stepped out onto the lawn of the restaurant where we landed, on the Chesapeake Bay. "I hope the other guests see me," she grinned. They did. Inside, we ate a dressed-up hamburger, got back into the chopper, took off, and returned to home base. So how did you like it, I asked Danielle. Fantastic, she said, "a once in a lifetime experience." What do you mean? "Well, to people like me this thing happens only once in a lifetime, if you're lucky." That sounded unnecessarily pessimistic to me. I told her to get back in, locked the door, and we took off again. Twice in a lifetime.

***

As for that Oxford English Dictionary, I sat down with its long-time boss after he had piqued my interest with something he wrote regarding pessimism versus optimism. Until his retirement, John Simpson was the Oxford's editor-in-chief. One thing I wanted to know was, how many words does the English language have? He had joined the staff of the world's most famous dictionary in 1976 as a young assistant, after his girlfriend had alerted him to a job opening, and the first word they asked him to sort out was *queen*. At the Oxford, they were working on a new edition to replace the original ten volumes from 1928, which had taken forty years to complete. Sorting out, that meant finding modern uses for a word, from after 1928, and by the time John joined the editorial staff, for the new edition they had progressed to the letter Q.

His employer soon realized that John Simpson was good at what he did. In all, he would work there for some thirty years, the last twenty as the chief. He wrote a book about it, *The Word Detective*, which was how we got to meet. His New York publisher had sent me a copy, asking if I was interested in talking to John. I read it, and said yes. For starters, he was the guy you ask: how many words are there? He was the authority, the language boss with, almost literally, the last word.

"Six hundred and eighty-five thousand." That is, if you don't count a bunch of isolated dialects. When you do, that would make it about a million. Follow-up question: of all those English words, how many does the average adult man or woman use? That couldn't really be measured with any precision, John said, because of each person's individual circumstances, but he estimated it to be twenty thousand, out of an average internalized vocabulary of between thirty and forty thousand words.

Three percent. Of all the available words, we don't use 97 percent. In fact, of 94 percent of all English words, English speakers don't even know their existence. All but one. I asked John: have you seen all 685,000 words come by at least once in your life? Answer: "Yes." That was inevitable, it was his job. John Simpson used to spend every single day collecting, organizing and explaining words.

Until he came home, which was the part that had intrigued me. Behind the front door, another world awaited. John and his wife Hillary have a daughter who can't talk. Not only that, she doesn't understand text at all. Their child has no vocabulary, period. "Four, five words," John said, "and even then you're not sure if she grasps it." Car, for example, he said, could just as easily mean the front door, or someone putting on a coat to go outside. Ellie Simpson is unable to communicate it. Her mental growth began faltering when she was six months old, and stopped completely at eighteen months. That's when a small child should be able to touch with their thumb every other fingertip of the same hand. Ellie couldn't do it, and she still can't now that she is in her thirties.

For parents, that is an, for lack of a better word, unspeakable tragedy. And for John, even more so. A life dedicated to getting everybody else to use language optimally, hits a brick wall at home. What does that do to a person's sense of pessimism? Fortunately, "she's happy in her own wordless world," but "there's nothing you can do."[23] And yet, "I always thought that one day I would be able to penetrate that. I'm still trying, because you should never give up." So there was the answer, from an optimist against all odds.

He discovered that Ellie's condition has a name, Angelman Syndrome, named after the pediatrician who first defined it in 1965. John Simpson has since added that term to the Oxford English Dictionary.

***

Words. Explaining something, understanding each other. We do funny things with how we use language, and it begins at an early age. This has been going on for a long time, so try to keep in mind that this is a book about optimism. The Brothers Grimm collected fairy tales, stories for young children. Their first edition included the fairy tale *How the Children Played Butcher with Each Other.*[24] Once upon a time there was a father who slaughtered a pig while his two sons were watching. When the boys went playing later in the afternoon, the oldest said, "You're a pig, I'm the butcher." He grabbed a sharp knife and stabbed it into his little brother's neck.

Mother, who was in the house bathing the baby, heard their screams, ran outside, pulled the knife out of her child and, in a rage, thrust it into the heart of the boy who had been the butcher. She then rushed back inside where she found that the baby had meanwhile drowned in the tub. Out of sheer despair she hanged herself. Father came home, saw that his whole family had died, and soon thereafter passed away from grief. No one lived happily ever after.

This was a read-aloud story for children. It was omitted from the Grimms' next edition, but that didn't make much difference. Their fairy tales continued to be loaded with dangerous witches, vicious giants, wolves that eat children, and vengeful stepsisters. From my own early childhood I remember a picture book about a boy who kept sucking his thumb after his parents told him not to. A monster pair of scissors appeared out of nowhere and cut off the thumb, blood everywhere. In color.

Fairy tales have been somewhat cleaned up over the last fifty years. But Hansel and Gretel still have a rotten stepmother who leaves them in the forest, and the witch still wants to cook and eat Hansel. Little Thumb still fights for his life with an ogre who meanwhile accidentally swallows his own daughters. Cinderella continues to be bullied at home. No matter which read-aloud story you pull out, it's about children facing an impossible and often cruel challenge.

Kids listen with rapt attention, even at a very young age, and want to hear the stories over and over again, endlessly. As they play amongst themselves, you see why. Things are brutal in children's rooms, with not only dogs but also sharks biting, parents running away, legs and arms breaking and needing to be splinted, dolls getting sick, and criminals a permanent threat. Back when my own daughters were little, video games didn't exist, but there was just as much bang-bang shooting going on. And when the oldest played a police officer, the youngest was the thief and she was mercilessly thrown in the slammer, for life.

Like optimism, the fantasy world of toddlers and preschoolers has long been fodder for inquisitive minds, especially pedagogues, educationalists and linguists. These children's fantasies do not even so much stand out for the often raw details of their content, such as trains running over young kittens, a bunny being burned alive, little boys murdering their entire families with bows and arrows or a cannon, or a hunter eating three babies.[25] They are especially notable for their common denominator. Young children, wrote New Zealand educator Brian Sutton-Smith, play-talk about "being lost, being stolen, being bitten, dying, being angry, calling the police, running away or falling down." They paint a world "of great flux, anarchy, and disaster."[26]

Reading to children is good for them because it helps develop their language. But for their fantasy world, it is hardly necessary. They pick up signals, images, information all around them, and transform them into fantasy worlds in which they themselves play the leading role.

Wait a minute, does that sound familiar?

***

So I worked at a newspaper for two decades, half that time as its executive editor, the guy where the buck stopped, responsible for all editorial content. That was an era when front pages grabbed attention with news about crime, traffic accidents, sex, and sports, and with what American journalism calls sob stories. Sex and sports because anyone can do it, crime and accidents because they might just happen to you, and sob stories because, well, ditto.

No one on any given day gives it much if any thought, but from all the information supply surrounding us we consistently and primarily seek out the coverage of events that happen by far the least often. Honestly, look around you, listen, a new baby is born to a family a few blocks down, a co-worker is getting married, the girl next-door, already a young woman really, is graduating from college, your aunt and uncle are making a cruise, your team won last night. Everywhere there's nice, sweet and happy news to watch, hear and experience as far as the eye can see, infinitely more frequently than what's going wrong. But good news we accept as normal and natural, rightly so, because it is. Instead, we mass-consume bad news. We snarf down reports of head-on collisions, murder, theft and shootings.

Why? It's not because we are collectively stupid and blind. It can make us feel pessimistic, yes, but that's not why we do it. We do this for the same reason we read to small children about getting lost, losing and killing, the same reason those children themselves play games loaded with horror motifs. After all, we also do it when we ourselves read a book or watch a movie. We then step into a fictional world that in reality does not happen to us, not now and most likely not ever, but it helps us to pretend. We actually grow by doing this, we become stronger. We learn, "without the potential staggering costs of having to gain this experience firsthand."[27]

Ask a child what she wants to be later, and she'll say: doctor, astronaut, mother, firefighter. Never you will hear one say: nothing, because I'll get a horrible disease or I'll die in a fire or I'll get eaten one day. The scary fairy tales and the horror play with other kids don't turn any child into a pessimist. Ask yourself after you watched Matt Damon getting lost on Mars, or after you looked away when the chainsaw killer went on a rampage in Texas, if that's what you yourself will be afraid of from now on, and you'll say, no.

No one who reads about a fatal traffic pile-up refuses to get into their own car next. No one who sees images of a plane crash somewhere far away changes their own travel planning. In 2014, the year when on July 17 flight MH14 from Amsterdam to Kuala Lumpur was downed by a Russian missile over Ukraine, more people boarded a plane at Amsterdam's Schiphol airport than ever before, 55 million. In 2015, that number grew to 58 million, followed a year later by 63 million passengers.[28]

***

When I show you the following figures, your initial reaction may be disbelief. But it's really true, we've all been scrutinized, studied and experimented on by that ever growing collection of curious scientists in all-revealing detail, and if you take a close look at your own average day, you can see it. We daydream. Endlessly. About anything and everything. About what we should have said or done yesterday instead of what we actually did. About how something went wrong, and the various ways it could have gone better in retrospect. About a success and how it came about. About an impending conflict at work, and how to approach it. About our marriage, about the kids, about someone else's marriage. Unless we are actively engaged in something that requires concentration, our brain wanders along an endless series of real or imagined scenarios.

The average duration of each daydream is short, fourteen seconds. At that point the thought associates itself to another scene. We have roughly two thousand of them, every day. That's almost eight hours, day in and day out, about a third of your life. The remainder you spend focusing on the job, event or action at hand, concentrated on and in the now, or you sleep, and even then you dream. You daydream as if you were a character in a story, beautiful, romantic, exciting, where everything comes true that you secretly want. Or it is a neutral film, about grocery shopping that still needs to be done, or about when you'll put the laundry in the dryer. Or it is a scary movie in which things go wrong. Your head, your brain allows it to happen, because nothing is really true, now. In the words of language expert Jonathan Gottschall, "While our bodies are always locked into a specific here and now, our imaginations free us to roam space-time."[29]

We do this for precisely the same reason that lets young children revel in playing their games loaded with danger, menace, heroism and idols. We practice, all our lives, on highly improbable scenarios. Our brain knows this. If you hook it up to a monitor, you'll see how the brain cells sympathize with you. Watch sex, and a whole series of brain cells participate. Watch a violent movie scene, and part of your brain reacts as if it were happening to you. But it has no effect whatsoever on the perfectly optimistic functioning of your subconscious brain. It knows, and informs you, that the real you will survive this fantasy with flying colors.

Optimism is, first and foremost, having faith in the positive outcome. It is not the absolute absence of moments of pessimism. After all, you practice your entire life on experiencing such pessimistic moments. But they are almost all made up.

Chapter 5

It all started with knives and table manners

The birth of optimism

How and when did optimism begin, and why? The answers actually make a whole lot of sense, and are also easy to map - literally.

The total land area between Alaska and the Argentine province of Antarctica contains nearly one-third of all habitable land on Earth, 31 percent. It is massive. In fact, the best way to imagine it is by looking at a globe, one that accurately represents proportions. There you see North and South America, the two continents stapled together by three bridges across the Panama Canal, and you realize how big it all is.

Close your eyes and imagine that all the land within that circumference is completely brown-green, covered by grass and forage. There are no cities anywhere, no people, there's no New York, Los Angeles, Toronto, Rio de Janeiro or Buenos Aires. There is only grass and crop. That's how large the world's land area is that we have deforested. It all used to look like Maine, which today is amazingly, and enviably, covered for almost 90 percent with young forest.

The massive deforestation didn't happen just since yesterday - it took our ancestors ten thousand years, since the end of the youngest Ice Age. The great-, great-, etc. grandparents, and their own great-grandparents, used a lot of wood. For building and for making tools, but mostly for having something to burn and to cook on. Wood was energy, and often still is. If gas, oil or electricity are somewhere not readily available, people cut down trees which then go up in flames.[30]

***

When we use the word "people," who are we talking about? Demographers calculate each year how many folks are populating the globe.[31] In 2020, there were nearly 8 billion. Estimates for the future are periodically adjusted, lately trending downward from earlier approximations. Nevertheless, they expect that there will be ten billion world inhabitants in 2060.[32] Is that enough, is that too much?

It depends on how you look at it. At that same university in Oxford, they love this kind of data. Eight billion people today, says Max Roser of the Our World in Data project, a number like that really only tells us something if we also look at yesterday and tomorrow. Our human species has been around for two hundred thousand years. That's the age of homo sapiens. It is a very rough estimate, but one that most scholars agree on.[33] They calculate that since the biological Adam and Eve of our species, 110 billion people have lived and died, in addition to the eight billion who are alive today.

This number alone should make us pause. You and I have been preceded in this world by over one hundred billion other people. That's three hundred times the U.S. population today.

It is five thousand times the population of the Netherlands, fifteen hundred times England or France, twenty-five hundred times Canada, twelve hundred times Germany, and one hundred times China or India. Each of them was an individual, as many girls as boys, all had thoughts, they knew hopes and fears, and they made plans.

Even if they only lived a short time, and had a thousand weeks to do something with their existence, or they lived to be eighty like we do today and had four thousand weeks available, they made plans beyond their chronological horizon. In the words of British researcher Oliver Burkeman, "We have been granted the mental capacities to make almost infinitely ambitious plans, yet practically no time at all to put them into action."[34] That does not and did not stop anyone from making such plans anyway. Everyone contributed to the future of the generations after them, even if they did not grow old at all and died as a child. Then their death drove their loved ones to look for ways to make life safer and healthier, and the odds of having to mourn such deaths smaller.

Why did they only start cutting down trees ten thousand years ago, and not much earlier? Answer: only then did our ancestors succeed in making fire and keeping it burning. They had obviously known what fire was for much longer, because they saw lightning strike trees and huts, and some watched volcanoes spew fire. They saw forests burn and their abodes go up in flames. They knew how to keep a fire burning for a while, and how to roast a boar while embers lasted. But lighting their own fire and making it suitable for cooking, that took until after the last Ice Age. Scientists have been able to verify this fairly accurately by examining the teeth of excavated skeletons.

No adult skeletons older than ten thousand years that were missing all teeth have been found anywhere in the entire world. But toothless skeletons of children from that long ago, yes.[35] Anyone who for any reason had lost all their teeth during childhood, because of vitamin deficiency or otherwise, could not chew and therefore could not survive. Only if they had at least a few teeth could they make it into adulthood. Prehistoric diets consisted of raw meat, plants pulled directly from the soil or from the tree, fruits often with thick skins and with stones, nuts, or raw fish. It required teeth.

Once fire became manageable, people learned to bake pots from clay. The first cooking pots date from ten millennia ago.[36] It was a revolutionary invention. Your nine-year-old who had already lost all her teeth suddenly didn't need to die of starvation. In a pot over a fire you now brought water to a boil, which meant that you could make a soup. Raw meat, tough plants, hard nuts - in a soup they became soft and swallowable. No teeth were needed for a soup, you could drink it instead of chewing it. Suddenly young toothless people could grow up and become old. Old, that was an average of 35 years at the most. Whoever reached the thousand weeks of a twenty-year-old was already middle-aged.[37]

The great awakening had begun. What had been unthinkable for nearly two hundred millennia was now suddenly possible. Boiling eggs instead of slurping them raw. Frying a steak, making applesauce, being able to choose between a hot and a cold meal. Manipulable food was a luxury of an unprecedented order. The new, quickly expanding brain was working at full capacity: what else is there that we always thought unthinkable? Optimism was born.

***

The year 10,000 BC is a safe starting point for writing the history of optimism. Studied heads who have dedicated their lives to sorting stuff out for the rest of us have by and large reached a unanimity about the end of the last Ice Age. Roughly twelve thousand years ago, they say. So we start a bit before fire was being brought under control, and before the cooking pot was invented. The brain was still underdeveloped, and everybody was still strutting around like the large two-legged digestive tract that in fact they were.

The worst inconvenience of all the ice was beginning to subside and was finally disappearing altogether. Man had been cold. They had discovered the hard way that sunshine alone was not enough to keep them warm, especially when hunting for animal fur to cover themselves with was no walk in the park, with frozen fingers and frozen feet. One attempt after another was made to control fire permanently. It took a few centuries, but once they got it down, they immediately moved on to discovering the next innovation. They were looking to invent something that could replace a hole in the ground.

What they needed was an object to heat water in, without it seeping away into the sand. Lighting a fire and keeping it alive was easy enough once they knew how to do it. But they couldn't use it to boil water, not in a hole in the ground, not without it disappearing. Until someone discovered that with the help of flames that they managed to keep burning at the bottom of the hole, they could shape and bake clay. After it cooled off, they found that water remained inside and did not leak away. This was the cooking pot, it happened ten thousand years ago, and it changed everything.

Especially for the mental capacity that enabled the brain to spawn bigger thoughts, ideas and plans. Cooked food, whether soup for toothless people or soft-boiled potatoes, vegetables and meat, requires a much less robust digestive tract. The breaking down of plant cells or boar meat tendons and muscles was no longer performed inside the stomach and intestines of the eater, but in the cooking pot. As the ice melted and fire allowed itself to be managed, people's bodies gradually outsourced that labor. As a result, the digestive organs shrank considerably.

Smaller intestines require less energy. In the human body, that energy went elsewhere, to the brain. That's where an average two percent of our body weight resides, but also where we expend twenty percent of our energy. Our brain is our biggest energy consumer, twice the amount of what is required by the entire stretch between esophagus and the body's exits.[38]

Have we as a species learned how to use that energy well? You bet we have. Optimism is a combination of hope, faith and confidence that we can bring about something better than what we have today, and make it last. Nestled inside the brain case that holds two percent of our body is a belief that everything can be made bigger, farther, faster, higher, deeper, smaller, more, less, healthier, more enjoyable, more comfortable and safer than we were used to through yesterday.

And so our ancestors invented the knife.

***

The knife, like cooking, roasting, baking and simmering on fire, has ten millennia under its belt. It is a nephew of its older uncle, the axe. Hand axes are very much older than the knife, at least by a million and a half years, or, according to a Chinese myth: the axe is as old as creation. A giant named Pangu, they say, stepped out of a cosmic egg with in his hand an axe.[39] He used it to cleave a hole between heaven and earth, to make room for his eyes. Those he then turned into the sun and the moon.

Axes have always had only one overall function: to break something, cut something off, cleave something in half, to chop something, or someone, to death. The hand was eventually replaced by a handle, which was not only safer for the user, but also added chopping power by increasing the speed of the strike. Other than that, nothing of significance has changed about the axe since the very first day.

The knife, in contrast, is pretty much the epitome of change. The first knives were made of stone, a shard of granite, quartz, flint, and those who lived in a volcanic area made knives from lava glass. Such knives were razor sharp, and they were fragile. What the ancestors sought and invented was a knife made of metal, of bronze, iron, and finally steel. Carbon steel, stainless steel, and from there to titanium and the ultimate to-day, molybdenum-vanadium.[40] Thin knives, large knives, flat, convex, tapered, one-sided, two-sided, with or without forked teeth attached.

A knife had to be able to dissect food ingredients, remove the skin from an animal, cut muscles and tendons. It had to be able to peel, deseed, debone, slice, ever finer, ever thinner. The sharper the knife, the healthier, better and more appetizing the meal. Ten thousand years of optimism history is first and foremost the story of ten thousand years of knives, of cooks and chefs who, with tireless optimism and unrelenting success, continued to search for ever better and ever more efficient food, for the benefit of ever healthier people in an ever more productive society.

But it is also a story that inevitably cuts both ways. For a knife that can feed can also cause to bleed. In the blink of an eye it may turn into a stabbing, slitting and slashing device. The last place you want to see that happen is in the bosom of the family, at the table where everyone gathers for the shared act of survival: the meal, eating, the collective rite of refueling the body. And therefore ten thousand years ago our forebears invented table manners, an etiquette that refined itself over time and produced a second incarnation of the original, the table knife.

Nothing symbolizes the clash between optimism and pessimism as acutely as the kitchen knife and the table knife. The desire to make one ever sharper and the other ever blunter flowed in both cases from a deep-rooted will to live healthier, longer and more comfortably. In a chef's hand, the knife can never be sharp enough. In the hand of a table companion, it must be harmless. Because cutting into ingredients is one thing, but cutting into a fellow diner is taboo. That's why the Chinese and Japanese use chopsticks.

Hence table manners. Rules of the game, agreements, compromises. Laws were originally table manners. They reflect a widely held optimism that, as long as we manage to control our demons, every dream can eventually be turned into a fact. And they work, on large and tiny scales, every day. Laws underpin our blind faith in what's inside the milk jar at the supermarket, in the pharmacy's pills, and in the functioning of traffic lights.

In all cultures, legislation is the ultimate result of what were originally rules of conduct at the dinner table, man-made agreements about the quicksand between feeding and protecting. Rules governing table knives that became increasingly blunt, that had to surrender one of their cutting edges, that lost their sharp tip and replaced it with something semicircular or oval. They were placed next to the plate with the sharp edge facing inward. Over time they no longer lasted a whole meal, bread was broken and not cut, cheese got its own innocent knife, and so did fruit, which was best pared with acidity-resistant silver.

The only reason why finally, at a relatively late stage, in Venice during the eleventh century, the fork was invented to join the knife, was that the rules no longer approved of knife tips lifting a bite of food to the mouth.[41] Also, not everyone enjoyed watching how at the head of the table the meat was being held down by unclean fingers while the carving knife divided the servings.[42] Hooray to the fork, as long as it sits next to the plate with the curved side up and the teeth down when not in use.

Every sword, lance, dagger, harpoon, bayonet, every bullet, torpedo and missile that pierces an enemy target is a derivative of the knife. Our ancestors had it figured out early on: if we are to have a future, we must all agree on seriously abiding to certain regulations. Reasonable people may differ among themselves as to how well or badly this has been applied over the centuries, but the facts speak for themselves.

***

Guus was an American, but he was born in The Hague. His grandfather had attended the Delft university, and left for America where he served as a general in Abraham Lincoln's army before becoming a wine merchant. Guus Bohlen married a wealthy German bride. He had a sailing yacht built that he named Germania. It was suited for ocean races that would sometimes stretch for weeks on end, which caused the kind of problems that such yachts often encountered. If the ship had a metal bow, over time it would corrode. This affected smooth sailing, but on top of that it cost money. Frequently, a rusty bow had to be replaced before the next long-distance race got started.

From his father-in-law Guus had inherited a shipyard. Engineers there were nonstop experimenting with new alloys for steel until they discovered that a combination of iron, chromium and nickel, together with a percentage of carbon, kept all rust out. The term stainless steel was born, and Guus had the bow of his boat covered with it.

At about the same time, another shipyard in Sheffield made exactly the same discovery. The combination of the three metals with an infusion of carbon brought something to life in the chromium, causing a protective film, invisible to the eye, to form around the steel, a layer that prevented degradation from without. In England too, they called it stainless steel.

Its availability proved to be a great step forward in a variety of ways. True connoisseurs prefer to use the term 'stain resistant' because under some conditions corrosion can still occur, for example when it comes into contact with strongly chlorinated water - which is why stainless steel is nowhere to be found around swimming pools. But it is perfect for ships and for construction. Skyscrapers are packed with stainless steel. So are outdoor trash containers, and the casings of nuclear power plants. It also works for kitchen countertops, since drinking water contains only a tiny amount of chlorine. Stainless steel has a very long life, it is easy to work with, and what's more, it can be fully recycled.

But Harry Brearley of the Thomas Firth & Sons yard in Sheffield had none of those uses in mind. He had been instructed to make better gun barrels so they wouldn't corrode anymore. And Guus from The Hague went by Gustav by that time. He had adopted his in-laws' family name, Krupp. They used the stainless steel for building cannons, and before long the gun barrels from England and the cannons from Germany were pitted against each other in two subsequent wars, the world's deadliest showdown since the invention of the knife.

Once all that was over, American, German, English, Italian, Russian and Japanese engineers took a good look at each other. They agreed that stainless steel had turned out to be a perfect material. They entered into a competition to see who could make the best stainless steel kitchen knife. Japan won. For a gyoto knife, just about any professional chef will easily fork over a thousand dollars, without blinking an eye.

Chapter 6

Random choices & freak hits and misses

Optimism when things go bonkers

One of the main imperfections that nature has saddled us with is that we know nothing with certainty about tomorrow and all the tomorrows thereafter. Every day, we enter the future blind. We consider it normal, it's all we know, and we hum along with Brian Wilson and the Beach Boys, "God only knows." But, religious or not, even that we don't know for sure.

Maybe every tree leaf knows in advance that it will change color as early as next fall before dropping dead within a matter of weeks. Perhaps the ocean knows that each day the exact same amount of water will continue to circulate in, on and above the Earth, infinitely, and that is why it crashes itself with such carefree abandon onto the rocks of the Scilly Isles. And the keys to my helicopter hanging from the arm of a two-dollar crucifix-Jesus that I bought at an auction one Saturday -

what do they know for sure? It is the same Christ image, arms wide, that is also looking out over Rio de Janeiro.

What we do know, on the other hand, is that in the absence of uncertainty there would be no optimism, because there would be no demand for it. Everything would then be certain, fixed, known, and everyone would be able to foresee and expect what will and will not happen. Nor would there without uncertainty be any hope, because hope too is rooted in the unknown. Pessimism? Perhaps, once you realize that everything is inevitable, unavoidable and inescapable.

But history shows convincingly that virtually nothing is and ever was set in stone. We're not talking about thunderstorms or earthquakes here, not about pandemics or ice ages. This is about moments that come with options for humans to choose from, yesterday, a hundred years ago, a thousand years ago. And it is the history of all those past crossroads where all hope and expectation have based their source. Specifically - and bear with me when at first glance this looks almost painfully contradictory, but I will walk you through the evidence - specifically the history of moments that went entirely wrong and bonkers.

This goes against all intuition, and also against the gospel that everything is predestined. But it is the reality, and reality speaks with clear facts. Leaving natural disasters and until-now-untreatable diseases aside, the vast majority of moments, events and consequences, good and bad, have throughout history been avoidable. This is another way of saying: they could also have tipped the other way.

They didn't, and for the course of history that's the only thing that counts. But the mere fact that they realistically could have, is what optimists have always picked up on. Whenever there are options for humans to choose from, the effects of any choice not made are avoided. Sometimes this is fortunate, sometimes not, but either way, almost nothing was and is inevitably set in stone. That's helpful knowledge the next time a similar moment arrives, because if the first time ended bad, the next time could have a different outcome.

So what kind of tipping moments are we talking about? Did they carry any weight as to how history has unfolded? Well, fasten your seatbelts.

For what would have happened if Leo Lojka had driven straight ahead instead of making a right turn? And what if Napoleon Bonaparte had waited just a little bit longer before dispatching his troops to the Dominican Republic? Similarly, what if Abraham Lincoln had had five more weeks of faith? What would the world be like if Guiseppe Zangara had brought a sturdier stool instead of a wobbly folding chair? Not to mention Willem Barentsz. What if he hadn't been so damn stubborn?

Leo was a chauffeur on June 28, 1914. He did not know his way around town, but all he had to do was follow the two cars ahead of him. The town was Sarajevo, his passengers in the back were Archduke Franz Ferdinand and his wife Sophie. The archduke was not just anybody. He was the designated successor to his uncle, Austro-Hungarian emperor Franz Joseph, who at 83 was a feeble old man, and not expected to stay alive much longer. In due course, the nephew was going to be the emperor.

There had been an attempt on the life of Leo's prominent passengers earlier that day, with a grenade thrown at the car, but it had bounced off and exploded under the vehicle behind them. The couple remained unharmed and the motorcade rushed to City Hall. There it was decided that Franz Ferdinand would forgo the original purpose of his visit, the opening of a new museum. Instead, he would go to the hospital to check in on the injured passengers from the other car, to bolster their spirit.

No one told the drivers in the motorcade how to get there. The mayor knew, and he would lead the way. But he was a nervous wreck after a very upset archduke had read him the riot act. Inadvertently, he allowed the cars to drive by the same spot where the grenade had been thrown earlier, and to turn right on that corner, exactly where one of the perpetrators was still standing on the sidewalk eating a sandwich, baffled to find his target right in front of him a second time. Leo was ordered to turn the Gräf & Stift automobile around, so he stopped the car, put it in reverse, and then the engine stalled. All the 19-year-old assassin had to do was pull the trigger. His two shots started World War I.[43]

***

Or get this one: at the dawn of the nineteenth century, in the year 1800, there was plenty of animosity going on between France and the young American republic. French ships persistently raided American merchant transports, capturing vessels and goods worth up to twelve million dollars, more than half a billion in today's currency. Napoleon had meanwhile ferried tens of thousands of soldiers to Hispaniola, the island that was half Haiti, half Dominican Republic. It was a rich island, at the time America's main trading partner after England.

Napoleon was interested in the Caribbean because he saw it as an alternative conquest territory. Spanish troops had already vacated the Dominican Republic, Haiti was also up for grabs, and France had made itself popular in the area by officially abolishing slavery. If Napoleon's adventure on the European mainland were to fail, he would still have at least as much room in the Americas to spread France's wings. Louisiana had recently become French territory again, after Spain had returned it. With enough military, there were a lot of hornets nests to be stirred there, in the backyard of George Washington, John Adams and Thomas Jefferson.

But by the time 1802 arrived, the *Aedes aegypti* landed at Hispaniola as well. It was a mosquito, the spreader of yellow fever, a mass murderer. More than eighty percent of French soldiers became infected and died from it. Within a few months, nothing was left of the French punch in the Caribbean, and Napoleon had to make a choice. Stir up the naval conflict with America even further, or make a deal with President Jefferson. For continued skirmishes he simply had not enough soldiers available, much less a strong enough force to invade Louisiana, therefore he decided on the deal. Napoleon Bonaparte sold a huge swath of French-owned land to Jefferson, almost a million square miles, for three pennies per acre.[44]

Had the mosquito ignored the island of Hispaniola, yellow fever would not have broken out there. That's not something Bonaparte could have influenced one way or the other. But he could have delayed dispatching as many military overseas as he had, he could have waited, there was no hurry, time was on his side. Napoleon's soldiers would then not have succumbed. In that case, the fact that France owned Louisiana gave him just as much of a claim on the American continent as the united thirteen states had. It would probably have been very tempting to do something with it.

Louisiana back then was not what today is the home state of Mardi Gras, cajun and jazz. It incorporated territory of fifteen later states, along the full length of the Mississippi River west bank, including Missouri, Iowa, Kansas and the Dakotas, all the way into Canada. With the temperament he possessed at the time, Napoleon could have invaded the fledgling United States with a decent shot at success. In that case the 555-ft tall obelisk in Washington, DC would now be the Bonaparte Monument, slavery would have been abolished sixty years sooner, and America would be speaking French today.

***

Patience? President Lincoln had little of it left in him when in June 1864 time came to get nominated for re-election. Gains on the battlefield in the fight to restore and preserve the Union had been evident but slow, and voters were beginning to show Civil War fatigue. Lincoln figured that he would need every vote he could get in order to finish the job of re-uniting the United States. In 1860, the Republican Convention had picked an able running mate from Hampden, Maine, senator Hannibal Hamlin. Though the two of them hadn't met until the day both were inaugurated, and vice-presidents were given little to say and do, nobody in the nation's capital doubted that Hamlin was the kind of guy you'd want to be a heartbeat away from the presidency, if the president were to become incapacitated. Death had visited the White House twice before, recently, in 1841 when president Harrison had suddenly died from pneumonia, and in 1850 again when president Taylor had been killed by food poisoning.

Yet Lincoln dumped Hamlin for a second term. He was concerned that his ticket wouldn't be strong enough with a New Englander as a running mate. New England could be relied upon to vote for Lincoln anyway, so instead he let the party convention know that he'd prefer a southerner for vice-president. He picked Tennessee governor Andrew Johnson who was then duly nominated and chosen on June 8, 1864.

Six weeks after the convention, July 22, Lincoln's general William Tecumseh Sherman won the Battle of Atlanta. It suddenly made a Union end victory all but inevitable, and boosted Lincoln's popularity. The president won his re-election overwhelmingly without ever having needed the balance that his Tennessee running mate brought to the ticket. The rest is history. Lincoln was assassinated six weeks into his second term,

Andrew Johnson became president, and he completely screwed up Lincoln's carefully planned reconstruction of the South.

So, what if Hannibal Hamlin had not been dumped and become president instead? Johnson pardoned Confederate military men and politicians by the thousands. He returned their possessions to them, and allowed them to restore the South's way of life in many ways to what it was before they seceded. Black people, though no longer enslaved, remained second-rate citizens. It would take another century, until the late 1950s and '60s, for the civil rights movement to successfully change the law. Most historians agree it's unlikely that Maine's Hamlin would had let it come to that.[45] He was a hardcore civil rights advocate who loudly challenged Johnson's policies.[46] President Hamlin could have spared generations of people with a colored skin the pain they continued to endure in southern states that had lost their slavery case fair and square. If only Honest Abe had been a tad more patient and not listened to his fear of suffering a loss that, in the end, was not forthcoming.

***

Again, the relevance of examples like these is not so much what actually happened, but that there were alternative outcomes that *could* realistically have happened. Driver Leo should, and could, have been told to take a different route in Sarajevo, which was the plan to begin with. Napoleon could have sent his navy off to the Caribbean later than he did. History shows that human optimism has thrived on the what-if phenomenon, especially in situations that ended badly. For if worst-case scenarios are not automatically only-case scenarios, if viable other outcomes were feasible even though at the time they were not attained, then the next time may actually produce a different result. Optimists have always clutched that straw, even in the worst of circumstances. And over time it has helped them to improve the world dramatically.

Here's another one for you to ponder, the opposite of what happened in Sarajevo nineteen years earlier. It was 1933, and Italian immigrant Giuseppe Zangara had been in the United States for ten years by then. He was a bricklayer, but in the early 1930s, with a totally collapsed economy, there wasn't much money to be made in construction. Zangara became poor and resentful. In November 1932, Franklin Roosevelt had been elected president which did nothing to change Zangara's pessimism. The Roosevelts were a wealthy family, and in his eyes the Great Depression was to blame on all rich people. On February 15, 1933, two weeks before Roosevelt was to take the oath of office, the president-elect came to Miami Beach. That was convenient, for Giuseppe was there, too. He was going to shoot Roosevelt.

His plan was nipped in the bud once he had unfolded his chair. Zangara was short, he stood only five feet and a half. In order to be able to see Roosevelt's car above the heads of other people on the sidewalk, he needed a step up. The moment he pointed his gun, his stool wobbled. Giuseppe Zangara fired six shots. Four bystanders were wounded, he missed Roosevelt, and instead hit another passenger, the mayor of Chicago. That shot was fatal.

What if it had been Roosevelt who was assassinated that day? He was on the eve of a presidency that would last twelve years. During that time, he successfully fought the Depression and led America and the world through World War II, on fronts in Europe and Asia. Had Zangara killed him, vice-president-elect John Garner of Texas would have become president instead. He favored limited government, he was against federal intervention in the Depression, against Roosevelt's New Deal social welfare plans, and against getting involved in foreign wars. The world would have looked massively different if stonemason Zangara had brought a sturdy stool instead of a wobbly folding chair.

***

History is a hodgepodge of random choices, and of freak hits and misses. Events that caused great consternation among the people that were affected. Had it not rained continuously in Ireland for three long weeks in the summer of 1845, there would have been no outbreak of potato blight. In that case there would have been no mass starvation, and a million Irish would have remained alive.[47] Or this one: if Julius Caesar had not allowed himself to be seduced when Cleopatra, 21 years old, came rolling out of a carpet, it was all but certain that she would after Caesar's death have left Mark Antony alone and, consequently, stayed away from her fatal flirtation with Emperor Augustus thereafter. Then Egypt would have likely remained a powerful empire for quite some time longer, and more importantly for the rest of the world, it would have made major contributions to world literature. Egypt was way ahead of everybody else, even the Greek, in mastering the art of writing. They were early users of papyrus, a plant that was native to Egypt only.[48]

Remember the Wilson couple in the White House? She was the bride who instilled in her groom a sense that he was pretty much Jesus' substitute on Earth, with all the resulting disastrous choices that followed at the end of World War I. By the time a crippled Woodrow was succeeded as president in 1921, it was too late to avert disaster, but that does not exonerate his successor - not in the context of what-ifs. After all, if on May 17, 1916 Ohio senator Warren Harding had not mailed a quick note to his neighbor's wife, then most likely he, not Wilson, would have been elected president of the United States that year. Neighbor Carrie was blackmailing him with his own love letters because she wanted him to choose her, not the White House. Harding quickly let her know that he caved, and that she'd get her way. He postponed his candidacy by four years, which was a calamitous decision.[49]

I am still navigating history's evidence with you, still answering the question about what the importance is of events that could have tipped the other way: "Did they carry any weight?" Events that accentuate how avoidable the seemingly unavoidable has often been, and why optimism has always deep down known this. Here's another one:

Rulers of the Italian city of Genoa in the Middle Ages prohibited Christians from exchanging money and making loans, let alone charging interests. They looked away when locals of other faiths did it, as long as it took place in the open air and in full public view. Jewish merchants took advantage of the opportunity. They sat on a marble bench, *banca* in Italian, in the church square and provided loans to other businessmen. If no one had enacted such a rule in Genoa, or if the merchants had sat down somewhere else and not on a *banca*, in a park, on a chair, or on the deck of a ship, who knows if today we would have a park account, a chair card, or a deck balance.

This in itself is innocent enough, but in France between the two world wars a sum of between four and five billion dollars was withdrawn from various bank accounts.[50] With that money, André Maginot built over a hundred military forts along the French border with Germany, at 10-mile intervals, each heavily fortified and guarded. Adolf Hitler would not dare attacking this defensive wall, Maginot insisted. He was correct. Hitler left it alone. Instead, the German army steamrolled through Holland and Belgium, ignoring the entire Maginot Line, and arrived in Paris unhindered, in no time. What if defense minister Maginot had made a second withdrawal from the banks, and built a second line of defense, this one along the Belgian-French border?

No one knows the answer to any of these questions, in part because they were not asked at the time. But each had to do with a choice made or dodged, and either way, a choice not made is also a choice. Often with far-reaching consequences. The famine in Ireland led, on balance, to one of the most successful waves of emigration in history. Cleopatra, daughter of an incest marriage and herself the bride of her two brothers, became immortally popular, and Egypt's unhealthy incest marriage tradition came to an abrupt end. In addition, from the ruins of two world wars rose a Franco-German friendship that inspired and underpinned a prosperity the likes of which Europe had never known before.

The initiative of France and the three Benelux countries in 1951 to enter into an economic cooperation with Germany and Italy, mortal enemies only six years earlier, resulted in what is today a political, financial and economic union of twenty-seven countries. It is, outbursts of Russian foolishness notwithstanding, today the best safeguard against barbarity on a continent that for centuries was the most violent in history.

Chapter 7

The fake Vermeer

Optimism vs. wishful thinking, 2.0

Pessimism has a nearby horizon, like a landscape with mountains. Rise above it, and the perspective widens. You see more, and you see proportions. The attempt on Franklin Roosevelt's life in February 1933 shocked everyone. But history, and the attacker's wobbly folding chair, tilted in the right direction. In Sarajevo, in the post office of the U.S. Senate and on the border with the impregnable French bastions, history tilted as well, but the wrong way, resulting in massive pain and a record number of war victims.

Those deaths can hardly be reasoned away with optimism, partly because the memory is too fresh. But time is one of nature's instruments that allow us to rise above it all, to widen our perspective. There is now a broad consensus among historians that the American Civil War, which well over a century and a half ago claimed more American lives than the two World Wars combined, had the effect of a much-needed, colossal cleanup. Once supporters and opponents of slavery had settled their deep differences by force, resulting in the setting free of four million slaves, an explosion of productivity and innovation broke out across the nation. Within fifty years, the U.S. became the world's largest economy, and it has maintained that number one position ever since.

And Willem Barentsz? He was a Dutch explorer who wanted to get rich. On May 18, 1596, despite two failed previous attempts, he stubbornly set out again from the island of Vlieland to find a northern shipping lane through Arctic ice. All trade lanes over water to and from Asia were southern routes, and they often took months to sail, at the expense of significant outlays of money. Via a northern route, Barentsz and his contemporaries reasoned, it would be much colder, but also shorter and less expensive.

Every attempt until then had been blunted by pack ice, no matter in what month of the year. Beyond the islands of Nova Zembla, Spitsbergen and Jan Mayen there was only ice, impassable. Barentsz tried again anyway, determined to find a passage, for if he were successful, Dutch merchants would make him very wealthy. Yet this third time he failed once more, and after four months of being stuck, ice shoves finally splintered his ship. Using the wood, his crew built a makeshift house on Nova Zembla, where they spent the winter together. With leftovers they made a sloop, and when the winter was over, they rowed away, hoping to find another ship that would venture this far north. They did encounter one, but by then Willem Barentsz had died, killed by scurvy.

Next, an Englishman was sent out to sea by his Amsterdam bosses, with the instruction to keep looking for that northern lane, but he decided to ignore them, no way, forget it. Henry Hudson sailed north far enough to be able to report that he had tried, then changed course and went west. He knew all about the Barentsz adventure, didn't feel like getting his ship crushed and splintered, much less dying from scurvy, so he made the turn and ended up at what is now New York. He discovered the mouth of a wide river that today bears his name, sailed upstream, and that's where the Dutch launched America's giant success story. The small island he passed just before he found the river, today known as Nantucket, was mapped shortly thereafter. It was christened Vlieland.

Hudson was an optimist, and obviously also a realist. Barentsz was no doubt an optimist as well, but mostly a wishful thinker. It took another three centuries until someone managed to complete sailing through a Northeast passage.[51]

****

So let's look a little closer at that paradox of realism versus wishful thinking. Back to our own century, to the helicopter, to twenty-six degrees of latitude below the equator. The small town of Chañaral sits on the coast of Chile, on the edge of the Atacama Desert. It is the furthest thing from a seaside resort. Sand and sea have long been polluted by copper mine waste, and no one risks swimming here. It has an airstrip. That's where we landed the helicopter on June 22, 2007. We needed to refuel.

Turned out Aeropuerto de Chañaral was abandoned, folded, closed. Boys were playing soccer on the runway. We set the helicopter on a cracked helipad, two of us kept the soccer players at a distance, the other went to check out the town. Chañaral is situated on what is locally identified as Route 5. Most other people know that two-lane road as the Pan American Highway, a roughly 20,000-mile freeway that runs intermittently from northern Alaska to southern Chile and Argentina. It is the longest street in the world.

For that reason, Chañaral has a gas station. The highway here is used mainly by bus and truck traffic between Iquique on the border with Peru, 500 miles north, and the capital city of Santiago, 600 miles to the south. The Shell station had a parking lot for large vehicles. The owner's name was Marco; he spoke English fluently, the effect of having lived in New Zealand for a year, he said. He offered us to park the helicopter on his property. In return, we were welcome to fill our two tanks with fifty gallons of his gasoline.

Robinson helicopters, like small planes, normally fly on a special high-octane, low-lead aviation fuel. When that is not available, as was the case that day in Chile, the engine will also run on lower-octane, unleaded car gas, provided it is ethanol-free. So I said yes to the offer, and we hopped the chopper from the abandoned little airport to the gas station a few hundred yards away. Marco cordoned it off with plastic tape and barrels. It was late June, winter below the equator, and the sun was sinking. We decided to spend the night in town. Marco promised continuous surveillance of the Robinson. I believed him.

Wishful thinking? There is no such thing as certainty, so I had to make a choice. The worst possible outcome was: this will be the end of the expedition. In the middle of the night someone's car could catch fire at the pump, and the flames could spread to the helicopter. Or someone would step over Marco's plastic barrier and damage the aircraft. In my mind, both possibilities seemed remote enough to not worry about it too badly, but even if I guessed wrong, all I would lose was a helicopter. In that case, the crew had to find a way to get to Santiago, catch the next plane home, and from there I would have to sort it out with the insurance company.

That was the worst case scenario. The best case was that nothing bad would transpire, and that we'd take off again without incident in tomorrow's daylight. The optimist in me went for the best case, and decided to leave the helicopter by the roadside in the middle of nowhere under the surveillance of someone else whom I had never met before. Of course, I could be hopelessly wrong. I could as a matter of fact be suffering from a bad bout of wishful thinking.

***

Obviously, I wouldn't have been the first, and for evidence all I had to do was to stay close to what I knew. In my Dutch newspaper years, I often drove on a road named Brediusweg, in the town of Bussum. It was named for Abraham Bredius and his parents who used to live nearby. One day in the year 1937, Bram was visited by a lawyer who showed him a painting. Bredius was considered a connoisseur of the arts, one of the best, acknowledged in particular as a Vermeer expert. The lawyer said, "My client believes this is a real Vermeer. It is called *Supper at Emmaus*." By that time, Bredius was already 82 years old, but once when he was a younger man, he had exposed a body of fake Vermeers. He had recently decided that he was now retired. His latest book, about two hundred fake Rembrandts, was finished and for sale in bookstores.

Bram Bredius didn't need much time. He checked whether the underlying canvas was from the seventeenth century, whether the paint was desiccated and hardened the way it should be after three hundred years, and whether the smaller details fit as well. Minutiae such as the pointillés on the bread, just like the bread on Vermeer's Milkmaid, the vase that all but clamored Golden Age, the entire scene the same way Italian master Caravaggio would have painted it. Bredius had suspected all his life that Johannes Vermeer had visited Italy and was tutored by Caravaggio. And then the paint itself, with all those old cracks in it. The Vermeer expert was deeply impressed. This was a real Vermeer. An early one, dating back to when the painter at the start of his career was still portraying biblical scenes. "Pristine," Bredius said.[52]

It was a forgery. The Boijmans Museum in Rotterdam paid half a million guilders for it, a value of ten million dollars today. No one noticed the paint had been treated with phenol formaldehyde. When heated for two hours, at a temperature of 220 degrees, it turns into bakelite, an early form of plastic. Rub it over young paint, and it will crack and dry, instantly hardening as if exposed to the passing of centuries.

The forger's name was Han van Meegeren. He was caught in 1945 after a faux Vermeer was discovered in Herman Göring's art collection, with the receipt still attached. Van Meegeren had sold it to Göring, and he was promptly arrested. Making money off top Nazis was treason, punishable by death. Realizing this, the forger hurried to confess, immediately turning it to his advantage. He said that he had been making fake Vermeers in order to rip off Hitler's right-hand man, as an act of resistance and, oh, by the way, the painting in Boijmans was also fake. Han van Meegeren became an overnight folk hero. He had fooled the Nazis, and also exposed elite art experts as nothing but a band of buffoons.

Reality was a lot more complicated than that[53], and after his death Van Meegeren lost quite a bit of his hero status[54], but the question that lingered was: what had possessed Abraham Bredius? How could he, the Vermeer connoisseur par excellence, a man carrying so much prestige in the art world, someone who had nothing more to prove, how of all people could he have arrived at such a spectacularly mistaken appraisal?

Bredius was an optimist, and he had every reason to be. He had become a confident man in the previous eight decades of his life, convinced of his own abilities. He was fully congruent with the three basic underpinnings of optimism: older age, professionally confident, and plenty of social contacts. Bredius was a man in balance. And in all the decades he had spent studying the life of Johannes Vermeer, his hunch had only grown that the painter had depicted more biblical scenes than the two that were known at the time.

At last, the crowning proof of his inkling lay before him: the missing link in the master's oeuvre, Supper at Emmaus. A work by the young Vermeer, therefore not easily comparable to his famous later paintings such as that milkmaid, the view of Delft or the young woman with the pearl, "yet every inch a Vermeer," a "masterpiece." He had difficulty controlling his emotions, he later wrote.

Abraham Bredius decided the painting was real because he wanted it to be real. Wishful thinking. Like Daniel Kahneman's investors on Wall Street, all wishful thinkers. Just like Annie Edson's expectation that her successful plunge over the Niagara Falls would make her rich. And also like Mrs. Jo van Meegeren who was home when the police came knocking. They had a search warrant and demanded to know if she herself had ever watched her husband painting forgeries. No, she stammered with her back to the fireplace. There, on the mantelpiece, sat the same porcelain that also appeared on one of Van Meegeren's false Vermeers.[55] She wasn't fibbing. Her brain wanted to believe it wasn't true. Wishful thinking.

***

In Chañaral, Chile, the helicopter crew woke up early the next morning. We had a long flight south ahead of us, a distance of five hundred miles, normally five hours of flight time plus another fuel break. The Robinson sat exactly as we had left her, with one little distinction. There were now families walking around the scene, parents with children. No one had ever seen a helicopter this up-close. It was Saturday morning, school was out, everyone had plenty of time to take family photos with the helicopter in the background. Our own photographer Sigurveig helped by pointing out the best angles. Marco came out of his office to reassure us. Chile was airing a television show that year centered around a helicopter, he said. It crisscrossed the country to surprise small towns with winners of prize money. The people of Chañaral thought we had descended from the sky to do just that.

To take off with a helicopter, you follow a simple procedure. You remove all obstacles, keep bystanders at a distance, start the engine, follow a checklist to make sure everything is working properly, make the rotor blades spin at full speed, and then you pick up the aircraft from the ground a few feet, in a hover. Once again you look around carefully, and you do a maximum performance take-off, straight up until you are above the surrounding structures and trees. Then you push the nose down, and enter into a forward flight.

I removed Marco's plastic tape and the barrels, pushed trash aside because otherwise it might blow into the rotor, and gestured bystanders to stay away. I waited near the tail rotor which spins six times faster than the two big blades and can chop an unsuspecting person into mincemeat. Everything was fine.

A helicopter engine starts like a car, with a key and a battery that sends a spark to the fuel via a starter motor. By now we had been on the road for seven weeks and had started the aircraft more than a hundred times. But it had been a freezing night, the oil in the cylinders was thick as molasses, and batteries don't have much patience for cold temperatures. Pilot Stephan's fourth crank attempt was followed by a loud bang, and then nothing. The starter had broken in two. There was no way that we'd be leaving Chañaral that day.

Chapter 8

The invention that changed everything

The great divide between optimism and pessimism

Whether a glass is half full or half empty often depends on a unique form of speed - the speed of change. Change in society, but also in the life of the individual. Fast changes tend to make people restless and insecure about what to expect next, which in turn affects an individual's, and at times also a society's, balance between optimism and pessimism. To get a sense of how this has played out over the course of the past ten thousand years, consider the entire timeframe as an athletic track of a hundred meters long. In sports, that's where they run a dash.

Here, the baseline is the day when prehistoric grandma and grandpa invented the cooking pot and the knife. The finish line is today. What you will see here is nothing remotely like a dash. That's because between start and finish actually almost nothing happens. The runners don't run, they barely walk, they shuffle. Change is slow. For millennia, only two paces rule, the speed of the wind and the speed of a horse. The world of generation after generation is virtually stationary and barely changing.

Horses determined the maximum distance of a day's journey. They were domesticated six thousand years ago, near the Black Sea, virtually simultaneously with the invention of the wheel. Goods and ideas were spread on horseback. There were also donkeys and oxen, and here and there the back of a camel or an elephant, but from Homer to Charlemagne to George Washington, everybody had the same average speed at their disposal. Over water, it was no different. The wind determined the speed of a ship. Ninety-five meters out of a hundred, on our athletic track, everything and everyone moves at the same pace.

Although, there was a brief flash, near the 80-meter mark. That's when the Romans figured out how to make cement and concrete. Water added to a combination of sand and a special type of limestone did not dissolve it but turned it hard as a rock. For a while this had noticeable consequences, as Rome's 2,000-year-old Pantheon with its concrete dome still demonstrates today: it lasts, it is sturdy, it survives the ages. Using their invention, the Romans constructed aqueducts and were able to transport water over land. They could build modern harbors, which led to new trading and transportation opportunities. In Rome two thousand years ago, there was a decent modicum of prosperity, and suddenly also a sense of how to record the speed of time: a sundial was stolen from the Punics in Catania on Sicily, the world's first clock.[56]

But the Roman empire collapsed and the recipe for cement and concrete literally went missing and remained untraceable for more than a thousand years. All the while, economic growth stagnated all over the Western world because no one was able to replicate the infrastructure that had been so successful in Rome. There were outliers here and there, later, parts of England and the Low Countries, because they had naturally navigable waterways[57], and we'll see in later chapters why in the late fifteenth century shipping merchants and bankers suddenly became very wealthy. But it wasn't until around the year 1820 that cement and concrete production was rediscovered.

This happened in the same decade that the train was born. Father and son Stephenson built a locomotive in England, and in one day moved five hundred passengers and a cargo of coal over a distance of nine miles. At first, curious farmers rode along on horseback on both sides of the tracks, but they soon couldn't keep up. Along the way, the train reached a speed of 24 miles per hour, a world record. A crowd of ten thousand people awaited the first passenger train at the terminus. The news spread quickly, worldwide.

Which was possible because at the 95-meter marker on our running track for the first time something really serious had happened. In the mid-fifteenth century, independently and almost simultaneously, goldsmith Johan Gutenberg of Mainz and Laurens Janszoon, a sexton in Haarlem, invented the printing press. There are plausible stories that someone in China had thought of something similar first, but true or false, it was the European event that had by far the greatest repercussions.

It's not that written texts didn't exist already; they had been in circulation for thousands of years. Merchants kept accounting ledgers, with debit and credit entries. Others wrote down stories. On parchment, on animal skin, or scratched into clay.[58] The Egyptian city of Alexandria even had a library of an estimated one hundred thousand books, written out on scrolls made of papyrus.[59] But almost always those were single-copy products. Anyone who wanted to multiply a text had to make a copy by hand. Therefore, ideas, thoughts, fantasies and factual news typically would barely spread at all.

Monks were for centuries the world's printers. They calli-graphed copies, mainly pertaining to the Bible, but an author could go to them with other texts if they wanted. The price for five pages was a florin, a gold coin worth, today, two hundred dollars. A 200-page book therefore would cost the customer the equivalent of eight thousand dollars, per copy. Not many people were reading in those days, mainly because they couldn't afford to read. And then suddenly came the real printers, men who rubbed ink over page frames with lettering in mirrored relief, and who made copies by pressing the frames against sheets of paper. Now a book with two hundred pages cost no more than thirty dollars, available in an unlimited run.[60]

This had stunning consequences, for even though the speed of daily life didn't change much, the speed of change did. Dramatically. Thoughts and ideas became portable. A book or a pamphlet could travel far, and reach perfect strangers, with never before seen effects. Those who previously might have found an audience the size of the local pub or the town square now had a large crowd at their disposal, just like that, at unlimited distances. In 1517, monk Martin Luther was the first to realize the scope of this. His 95 grievances against the Church of Rome were not only nailed to a German church door. They also went to a printer. With an estimated print run of 300,000 copies, Luther unleashed the world's first informa-tion revolution.

It ushered in a change that was welcomed by many, but that also went too fast for a lot of others. When considering the Reformation, one always looks first at how rulers reacted, the pope, cardinals, the king of Spain, and later pastors and politicians. But they had a direct interest, often related to maintaining or obtaining power. Ordinary citizens, including many who for personal reasons preferred to remain Roman Catholics, mostly stepped on the brakes. Things were moving too fast, their world was changing too fast. It left them inse-cure about what to expect next. The invention of the printing press resulted in the first great divide between optimism and pessimism.

Not that this made much difference for what came next. Once change gets going, it never slows down. It only speeds up.

***

Three centuries after Gutenberg and the sexton, in 1746, abbot Jean-Antoine Nollet in Paris summoned two hundred of his Carthusian monks to form a long snake line. Each monk had in one hand a 25-foot-long iron wire that the man behind him was also holding, and with the other he handed a second wire to the monk in front of him. Nollet was not only a man of the cloth, he was also a scientist; he had studied physics. He had been to Leyden University and had seen how students stored a high-voltage charge in a capacitor, basically a bottle of water with an electrode at the top. Abbot Nollet gave it the name Leyden Jar.

He had connected a group of such bottles so that together they formed a sizable battery, and he tapped it with the first monk's iron wire. All two hundred unsuspecting friars simulta-neously received an electric shock and fell over, squealing un-biblical syllables. In all, their line measured a mile. The abbot concluded he had established beyond doubt that electricity travels at a high speed.[61]

Roughly a century passed between Nollet's test and Samuel Morse who invented the Morse alphabet. During that period, inventors increasingly sensed that it was going to be possible for people to communicate with each other over a long dis-tance, directly, without loss of time. The written word, how-ever spectacular now that it could be printed and transported, was one-way traffic. Being able to reply immediately, as in a conversation, regardless of distance, that would really rock the world.

The telegraph was originally called a tachygraph, after the Greek word for speed, because the primary concern of the early researchers was the speed of the message sent. There was uncertainty about what the attainable length of a talk-back distance could potentially be. Abbot Nollet assumed that electricity transmitted indefinitely, but soon others discovered that voltage tended to decrease along the way. Hence, early telegraphs used only what was best compared with smoke signals.

The first telegraph consisted of two buildings, two pairs of binoculars, a set of wooden panels and two notebooks with codes. The distance between the two stations was ten miles, and the view between them was unobstructed. The panels were painted black on one side and white on the other. Thus, by making combinations of panel movements, the sender of the message could spell, letter by letter, what they had to say. The first telegraphic message from the northern French town of Brûlon read, "If you succeed, you will soon bask in glory."[62] The text took four minutes to travel, fifteen times faster than by stagecoach.

In no time, telegraph lines appeared, a series of terminals each of which was always within binocular range of the next station. There were fifteen between Paris and Lille covering a distance of 125 miles. Another line was established between Paris and Strasbourg, followed by proposals to build one to Amsterdam as well. These were the days of Napoleon Bonaparte who was interested, but when someone suggested that stations should transmit news as well, for consumption by the general population, he balked. Broadcasting the national lottery numbers, that was okay, but only because it could help to curtail fraud, which would save the French state money.

Anyway, by the time the first trains started running and the rediscovery of cement allowed the construction of concrete infrastructures, Europe possessed an extensive telegraph network of stations that provided each other with information by exchanging visual signals. Between Paris, Perpignan, Toulon, Amsterdam, Brest and Venice, and through smaller networks around other cities, nearly a thousand telegraph stations relayed to each other the message that a train carrying five hundred passengers had reached a speed of 24 miles per hour in northeastern England.

***

What we are looking at here are in essence the various degrees of humanity's adaptability to change, to transformations. How they react to changing circumstances, changing surroundings, to changing tools that in and by themselves advance the change, and to changing paces of life. When finally the great breakthrough of change occurred, with the introduction of the printing press, it unleashed one wave of disrupting innovation after the other, with an ever faster speed.

Not everyone did, or does today, adapt to that equally well.

So for the first time the world had an internet, two hundred years ago, at our track marker 98. The fact that manual signals were soon replaced by cables, and letters by morse, and that eventually the entire world came into contact with each other via first the telegraph, then the telephone, radio and television, and now via the internet that we all have at our disposal since three decades ago - these are, to some extent, details. The period between the first telegram, "If you succeed...," and the thousand stations that announced the end of the horse era was also thirty years. Halfway through, Claude Chappe, the sender of the first message, concluded that "...you will soon bask in glory" was not going to happen. He jumped off the roof of the telegraph building in Paris.

Claude Chappe had initially been an optimist in a world full of blinders. The eighteenth century in which he was born knew only those elementary speeds of the horse and the wind. People were ignorant of what was happening a hundred miles away unless they read a book about it, or eventually a newspaper. But news was never new, for it was already old and outdated by the time it was carried across a distance. That ought to change, Chappe sensed. Surely a way could be found to speed up communication, and he set out to resolve the challenge.

Sam Morse was born the year Claude Chappe sent his first telegram, in 1791. Sam was a portrait painter and he was four days of travel away from home when he mailed a letter to his wife Lucretia with the closing line, "I hope to hear from you soon." The next day he received a letter from his father informing him that Lucretia was dead. By the time he arrived home, Mrs. Morse had already been buried.

Despite his grief as a widower, he was as much of an optimist as Chappe. Morse considered it conceivable, and therefore possible, that people "in matters close to the heart" would become capable "of getting a man to his wife's deathbed on time."[63] He knew of attempts to electrify telegraphy, and he also knew that by then power could travel for miles, in the blink of an eye. "If it can travel ten miles without interruption, I can make it travel around the world," he said, and he got it done. Without complicated codebooks. Sam Morse visited a print shop, and counted the number of letters in the letter trays to see which ones were being used the most. Hence the *e* got the shortest Morse code, one dot. The *t* got one dash, and the *j*, the *q* and the *y* became the longest.

In the hundred years between abbot Nollet and painter Morse, the whole business of fast-messaging changed, faster and faster. Claude Chappe thought that, as the world's first telegrapher, he could exert some kind of control over change and innovation, and he was wrong. Dozens, soon hundreds of other researchers, scientists and inventors were building on the idea of communicating over distance, more often independently of each other than not. This went way too fast for Chappe, himself briefly a speed champion. He tried to apply the brakes by seeking official government recognition for his discovery, but did not get it. It turned him into a pessimist. He was 41 when he ended his life.[64]

***

Fast forward to the 100-meter mark, to our time. On April 19, 1965, Gordon Moore, the future founder of Intel Corporation, predicted that computer production and capacity would double every year. He adjusted his estimate after a while and made it two years, but regardless, he was right. Moore was talking specifically about semiconductors such as transistors, but his assertion, since known as Moore's Law, now covers the entire computer world. The scope of what computers and their individual components can do has been expanding exponentially for more than half a century. As has the number of scientists scattered around the globe. Ninety percent of all graduated smarty pants the world has ever produced are alive today.[65] Ninety percent, computer users one and all.

Gordon Moore might as well have applied his law retroactively, too, to cover the history of technology in general. Because as soon as mankind went full throttle at the 98-meter mark, the world changed beyond recognition. Urban and port construction were modernized, and in the U.S. future metropoles such as Chicago, Atlanta, Cleveland, Memphis and Miami sprang up. Those who moved to cities made themselves dependent on others, deliberately, for providing goods and services that, in rural areas, each family had been used to taking care of themselves, resulting in even more radical waves of innovation.

I live in Maine, in the largest congressional district by area east of the Mississippi. Bangor is the home of Stephen King, and his semi-haunted house with the big fence, with cast-iron spiders and bats welded to it, is a draw for tourists. King is popular because his stories distract from everyday. In Maine, everyday for the longest time, for many, meant logging, paper mills and fishing boats. Timber lorries on 18 wheels, unlimited lobster trapping at sea. Children in yellow school buses.

At first glance, all of that still exists. But a paper mill no longer employs an entire town. Much has changed from Millinocket once producing the nation's newsprint to Maine today being America's number one toothpicks manufacturer. Robots now do much of the labor. Air quality detectors intervene when smokestack emissions cross a line. Loading logs requires barely any manpower anymore. Drivers are prepared for soon-to-arrive days of steering their trucks from a windowless room, stationary, from behind a computer screen. School children are not taught calculus. They learn how to outsource it to their smartphones and classroom computers. With a mouse and a click, they can opt to speak Spanish. Or German, Japanese, French, because Google or DeepL translate their English. And eyes in satellites monitor whether the lobster fisherman is sticking to his strict catch limit.

Their daughter comes home to tell Dad and Mom to put a camera in the front door keyhole which will also turn on and off all the light switches in the house. She wants a refrigerator that warns when the soda bottle is half empty. And she asks Santa for a trans Barbie doll, because they are the new Elmo. Her watch tells her she took three thousand steps today. She taps it and quickly emails her steps report to her friend. She is eleven.

In my rural neighborhood, in the district where I live, where Donald Trump, unlike in the more urban rest of Maine, won a majority of votes, neighbors are slamming on the brakes. This is all going too fast for them. The world is going to hell, they fear, not even in a hand basket for those have quietly been replaced by online shopping carts. They consider their own world scarcely manageable. Between my fence and Stephen King's, a half hour away, blue flags in people's yards stubbornly insist that their man has won the 2020 election, and not Joe Biden. Their candidate, they believe, stood for halting the transformation of their world, or at least for slowing down the pace of the change. These people, my neighbors - good luck convincing them it's all going to work out.

Which is, to say the least, remarkable.

Chapter 9

Joe, Jeff, and the underappreciated luxury

Optimism and disruption

The neighbors see and do the same things I do and see. They drive to one of America's 75,000 banks, stick their debit card in the slot, press a few keys, and pluck their dollars from the wall. They stop at one of the nation's 67,000 gas stations, do the same thing they did at the bank, but gasoline comes out of a hose instead. If they drive an electric car, they charge it at one of the 46,000 charging stations. Some of them can be heard complaining. Why there aren't many more charging ports already, and why don't they charge faster.

They have long since stopped having a land line at home, much less a dial phone, and instead they have smartphones, on a family plan, one for each household member. They use it to pay at the Taco Bell drive-through for their burrito, which they watch coming down in a food elevator for them to grab. If they are over 62, they receive their social security by automatic deposit every second Wednesday of the month. They can see this on their phone, and if that puts a smile on their face, they take a selfie, for folks at home.

In that home, on average they have two laptops, a printer, a usually large refrigerator, a freezer, two TV sets, remote controls, a microwave, a propane or electric stove, a washer and dryer, a vacuum cleaner, a sound system, a hair dryer, a mixer, a blender, a coffee maker, a dishwasher, audio earbuds, a WiFi modem, one or more e-readers, a sewing machine, air-conditioning, central heating and electric toothbrushes. On average, every American adult has their own car on the drive-way or in their garage.

When they are old enough to remember what life was like fifty years ago, they realize the difference. But you have to ask them about it, because they themselves hadn't noticed it right away. It happened gradually. Fifty years ago, the average family income in America was $13,700. Half a century later, in Maine it was $78,000[66]. Growing gradually. The traffic fatality rate was 28 per 100,000 back then, but although it got much more crowded on the roads since then, it also got a lot safer: less than 12 deaths per 100,000 road users. Life expectancy rose from an average of 72 years to 79 during that time, in part because smallpox, polio, rubella and measles completely dis-appeared from the country during that same period thanks to successful vaccination programs. And girls and young women have meanwhile been allowed to compete on athletic fields. As a result, women's soccer in America often draws fuller sta-diums than when the men come out to play.

Gradually. And therefore not noticeable enough for the brake-slammers to count their blessings. But if you would have exposed them to the oft-cited Pinker speech when they were young, how would they have reacted?[67] Canadian Harvard psy-chologist Steven Pinker graduated in 1976 and, in retrospect, asked himself what he would have thought if someone had made a prediction back then.

What if someone in those days had looked thirty years ahead, one generation, and said that, yes, there would be wars here and there, but absolutely no third world war. That the Soviet Union would dissolve itself without a shot being fired, and that China would open its borders to practically unlimited worldwide trade. What if it had been predicted at the time that East Germany, where one in 160 citizens quietly worked for the Stasi secret police[68], would cease to exist, and that smiling students with hammers, axes and chisels would chop down the Berlin Wall. That the generals in Greece, Portugal and Spain would all give up their dictatorship, and that the president of Egypt would come to the Knesset and hug Israel's prime minister. Oh, and there was a black man locked behind bars on Robben Island in South Africa, but he would end Apartheid, pretty much single-handedly.

Such a prophet would have been ridiculed as an incorrigible optimist, airhead level. Yet the optimist would be proven right. Even though all these neighbors in Maine are slamming the brakes as hard as they are, change has made their world a much better place than it was fifty years ago, let alone a century or more.

***

When I was a teen, I overheard my sister's boyfriend telling my mother, with excitement in his voice, that there was going to be a phone installed in his family's home. Mom said she thought that was nonsense, "What do you guys need a phone for?" The boy had no good answer that I can remember, but since we're talking about change, phones, as we saw earlier, are a perfect microcosm.

Joe Engressia was five when in 1954 he discovered that he could make phone calls to neighbors by rapidly clicking the hook. Each digit of a phone number corresponded to a certain number of hook clicks. For a kid like Joe, this came in especially handy because he was born blind. He lived with his parents in Richmond, Virginia, and phone companies there soon began experimenting with buttons instead of a dial. You'd hear tones instead of clicks on the line. Even more perfect for Joe.

By the time he was nine, he had developed a perfect pitch. Joe could whistle like a piccolo, perfectly in tune and, critically, at a frequency of 2,600 hertz. He discovered that he could disconnect a call by blowing a certain whistle tone into the phone, to which the phone company switchboard system automatically responded by giving the caller unlimited freedom. In that vacuum, Joe could call any other phone number in the world, free of charge, by whistling it. Blind Joe Engressia did this flawlessly, and he did it often and with abandon. He was the world's first hacker, at a time when there was no internet.

Joe changed his name to Joybubbles, and when he went to college, he endeared himself to his fellow students. He sold long-distance calls of unlimited duration for a dollar a pop, simply by whistling into the mouthpiece for a few seconds. It enabled him to pay for any food and drinks he felt like ordering in the college cafeteria, and then some. He eventually ran into trouble when a phone company technician in Canada figured out what was happening, and Joybubbles was fined and expelled from school.

But because everyone liked him so much, and many also thought it was pretty neat that a blind young man with an IQ of 172 could bend the entire international telephone system to his will, the punishment was rescinded. Joybubbles graduated as a philosopher and became a pastor in his self-founded church, the Church of Eternal Childhood.[69] He read weekly

changing funny stories to children who called the Zzzzyzzer-
rific Funline.

***

Joe Engressia could serve his student customers only because they knew how to look up the phone number they
wanted to reach. In the Stone Age of the previous century
people got such information from a phone book. It was a useful
thing, and the only reason Joe gave his funline its name was
that it guaranteed he was the very last entry on the very last
phone book page, and that therefore everybody could easily
find him.

The old phone book is now dying. The very first copy was
printed in New Haven, Connecticut in 1878. It was not a book
but a piece of cardboard with a list of fifty names and addresses, without a corresponding telephone number. It listed
three doctors, two dentists, eleven other individuals, and the
rest consisted of stores and businesses.[70] The list was published by the local telephone company. The directory itself
made no money, but the phone calls did, because you had to
call the operator in order to be connected, and they charged.

Later this changed, starting when the Yellow Pages began
to appear. A directory publisher could now make money off of
it. Telephone subscribers could advertise inside, or get noticed
quicker through a bold printed entry. This is all now largely a
thing of the past, and for those who earned a fat living from
paper telephone directories, the world has changed negatively.

They are not alone. A similar fate befell the makers of en-
cyclopedias, replaced by Google. True, you can today look up
any entry that used to be in the paper Encyclopedia Britannica
with a simple mouse click, but browsing is a problem now that
you don't chance as easily upon names, things or facts you
were not specifically looking for but that you stumbled upon

while turning pages. It's a thorn in the side of the old encyclopedia creators.

It's also the tide of history. Many a bookstore owner who is now without a bookstore went through the same thing. In 1998, America still had twelve thousand such stores. Now that number has been cut in half. The main culprit? Amazon, deliberately given its name by founder Jeff Bezos so that it would appear alphabetically at the top of search machine results, at Lycos, AltaVista, Magellan, all since driven off the road by Google.

As we saw, not every innovation is an improvement, at least not for everybody. Reason: innovations disrupt, all of them do. It may be small-scaled or large, but always the old is cut loose and eventually replaced by the new. Anyone who loses something in this process may momentarily lapse into pessimism. Which would obscure an in itself simple given: human history is a succession of permanent disruption. And behind every disruption there was a man or a woman, or more than just one, who optimistically figured that they could change the world for the better.

***

Jeff Bezos had a job on Wall Street that he didn't much care for. He knew something about computers, was unstoppably restless, quit his job and, together with his wife, loaded their entire belongings into a moving van. Where do you want us to drive it, the movers asked, what is your new address? Bezos said they should take Interstate-80 and head west until further notice. This allowed him to think about it a little more, and he would let them know which way to go by the time they got to the interchange with I-90 in Ohio. By then Mrs. Bezos and he would have decided whether they wanted to live in San Francisco, or shoot instead for Seattle.

While on the road, his mind was building a virtual book-store. Bezos named it Cadabra. For a merchant, books are an ideal product. They ship easily, they don't break in transit, and they are about everything so you don't necessarily have to specialize. America in 1994 counted many large bookstores, including chains such as Borders, Waldenbooks, and Barnes and Noble where an enthusiast could spend hours. But each brick and mortar retail space came with its own restriction: by default, there was a maximum limit to the number of books they could display. Only the very largest stores had enough shelves to hold, like the legendary Library of Alexandria did, a hundred thousand books. A virtual bookstore on the internet had no such limitation.

Jeff Bezos started talking out loud about Cadabra while he was still traveling.[71] Others listened and thought they heard him say Cadaver. That wasn't good, and Bezos went looking for an alternative. He chose a synonym for unstoppable, *relentless*, and immediately reserved the relentless.com domain name.[72] But after he spent a few days checking the search engines to see if they had already picked up on it, he decided it took too long for a user to find his site. The internet was still function-ing too alphabetically for his taste, search engines were like a phone book, and so Bezos did what Joybubbles had done, but in reverse. The name Amazon guaranteed him a spot on the first page, at the top of the search results list. An added benefit: the Amazon is relentless too, in addition to being the biggest river in the world. Jeff wanted to make Amazon the world's biggest store.

So far, he has largely succeeded. Customers can, at home sitting on the couch, or in bed, or standing in the kitchen while preparing dinner, choose from more than thirty million differ-ent books, they can check out right there and then, and start reading immediately on their phones, laptops or e-readers, or have the book shipped and home-delivered. The physical world of brick-and-mortar bookstores would require three hundred Barnes and Nobles to match that. And even then you'd not be done, for books make up less than ten percent of what's available in the Amazon store. In fact, the selection has indeed become unstoppable: clothes, shoes, music, jewelry, food, toys, car tires, watches, lamps, garden furniture, the list is as endless as it is relentless, more than 350 million different items.

There are those who regret that in most towns the bookstore around the corner has disappeared. I am one of them. But that doesn't get in the way of the facts: shopping has become a whole lot more convenient since at the Elyria, Ohio interchange Jeff Bezos decided to follow Interstate-90 to Seattle. Because the internet's marketplace is now crowded with storefronts for shopping. Such as the used Subaru that's now parked on my driveway, bought unseen, from Carvana, for a while the Amazon among car sellers. It was sitting in a showroom a thousand miles away.

Chapter 10

The jackpot and the mighty chess queen

The optimism of love and getting married

Which is more likely, crashing in a helicopter, or winning the lottery? As long as you're grounded with a broken starter, there's no need to fear the crash. But if everything is working properly, the odds of getting involved in a helicopter crash are one in ten thousand flight hours.[73] Hardly anyone outside the military collects ten thousand hours in a helicopter. This is partly because there are very few civilian helicopters world-wide, less than thirty-five thousand. That's five helicopters for every roughly one million men and women. If automobiles were as scarce a means of transportation, there would be only forty cars driving in New York, ten in all of Paris, and fifteen in Berlin. It makes your chances of flying ten thousand hours minuscule. Good news.

And the jackpot? No particularly good odds either, one in 290 million. Even slightly worse if you play the Mega Millions: one in 300 million. Which doesn't stop many people from trying again next time, though, especially after someone in Lebanon, Maine hit it rich in a January 2023 drawing, at 1.35 billion dollars the second largest win in lottery history. As for the Powerball lottery, 45 of the 50 states work together, doing three drawings each week, every Monday, Wednesday and Saturday. State politicians are happy to endorse lotteries because they're a lot more popular than the alternative, raising taxes. A good portion of lottery revenues goes to the state government, which uses it to maintain roads and build schools, money that, unlike taxation, is voluntarily and spontaneously donated.

Because one never knows. On March 30, 2005, 110 people won a Powerball prize. The law of probability dictated that there should have been four or five winners, but one after another they began calling in, each reporting to lottery headquarters that they had five of the six numbers correct. A coincidence? Cheating? Nope, all had used numbers they had found in a fortune cookie. Only the sixth number was off, which is why no one won the jackpot, but the cash prizes of between a quarter and half a million dollars were well worth it.[74]

Fortune cookies fuel optimism, and at the same time they are the result of it. Contrary to what most people think, they have their origins not in China, but in California. In Hong Kong, they are marketed as "the one and only American fortune cookie."[75] A family business called Wonton Food in Brooklyn produces by far the most, invents the text and has a computer randomly come up with lottery numbers. The text on the little snippet with the winning March 2005 lottery numbers read, "All the preparation you've done will finally be paying off."

Many people keep them for a while, in their wallet, at the bottom of their purse, or on their nightstand. Not by some unwritten mutual agreement; it happens intuitively. The winners that day in 2005 had received their fortune cookie from 110 different Chinese restaurants, weeks earlier, and all had kept their slip of paper. America counts over fifty thousand

Chinese restaurants, more than all the hamburger restaurants combined. At the turn of the previous century, Chinese immigrants were mostly denied the right to work, and for years they were treated downright badly. Except when it came to cooking and cleaning, which according to most men in those days were not real jobs but women's work. And so Chinese immigrants in America started dry cleaners and restaurants everywhere - and I mean, everywhere. Even the boarding house in Washington, DC where John Wilkes Booth once plotted Abraham Lincoln's assassination is now a Chinese restaurant, by the name of Wok-n-Roll.

***

The helicopter crew ate Chinese that evening in Chañaral, and the next evening again, at the town square, after a barbecue lunch at gas station host Marco's home. Chinese menus are served all along the Pacific Coast, from Alaska to Argentina - the entire North and South American continent sometimes smells more like noodles, fried rice and fu yung than barbecue. All the while, the helicopter sat like a clipped bird in the Shell station parking lot, still a neighborhood draw. A mechanic was on his way from Santiago, in a bus that took fourteen hours to cover the distance. He brought a new starter. And sure enough, two hotel nights later I found Julio under a half-peeled helicopter, tinkering with her bowels.

Helicopters are as miraculous as are hummingbirds, bumblebees and dragonflies. They can stand still in the air. A bumblebee makes two hundred wing movements per second, a hummingbird no more than fifty, and a dragonfly only thirty, all due to the ratio of wing span to body weight. A bumblebee is relatively heavy and needs four wings to enable them to hang still for a few seconds, then they must again move forward in order to avoid falling. A hummingbird is light. It lasts considerably longer in a hover and can also fly backwards if it wants. Dragonflies are the ultimate. They weigh less than a gram and are by far the best predators in the animal world, with a success rate of 97 percent, five times better than a lion. No wonder dragonfly tattoos are favorites among female helicopter pilots. The Bell helicopter that the Maine forestry service is using out of Old Town has a dragonfly as its logo.

The bee, the bird and the insect have been able to do for hundreds of thousands of years what aviation has only been capable of doing for one mere century. Cause air to flow quickly across the top of a wing, faster than along the bottom, so fast that it creates a pocket of air pressure that is lower than what's below the wing. It's like the weatherman always says: stronger winds create lower air pressures. And because a high air pressure naturally moves toward a lower one, it creates under the wing an upward force. That's how an airplane stays aloft, why a hummingbird does not fall, and why there are helicopters and their offspring, drones. The difference with an airplane is solely that a plane's so-named fixed wing does not move, whereas the rotor of the helicopter does. Without forward speed, there is no airflow over an airplane's wings, and therefore there's no lift. A helicopter can hang still, for hours if necessary, because it causes its own airflow.

Julio showed me the broken starter. The outer skin was completely cracked. Within two hours he had replaced it with a new one. Give it a test run, he suggested. The engine did indeed start, but again it came with a loud bang. The new starter also broke. Don't turn it off, Julio warned, because as long as the helicopter's main engine keeps running, no starter is needed. The distance we had to travel that day was five hundred miles, five hours of flying. It required a stop somewhere midway for refueling, but if we were able to find an airport where we could do a hot fuel, which means filling the tank while the blades continue to run, there would be no need for a restart.

And that's what we did. We left the welcoming but otherwise unforgiving parking lot of a dusty gas station on the longest road in the world behind us. Off to the airstrip near Valparaiso where Julio's hangar stood. There, all necessary repairs could be made in a professional environment. Julio himself went for a nap. His bus home wouldn't leave until that evening. He deserved his sleep, for he had made the right call. The helicopter's engine didn't fail that day. We got the hot refueling done, and reached our destination without further incident.

***

Why am I telling you this? Not only because it is highly unusual to lose the same engine part of a helicopter twice, let alone at a spot in the world where in a thousand-mile radius no helicopter mechanic can be found other than the one we managed to reach. But I also had a private reason for hoping that the thing could be repaired as soon as possible.

I was in love. Way over my head. I had been dating her for six months by the time I took off in Maryland and watched her getting smaller and smaller as we waved goodbye at each other. By now I was halfway through our expedition and I hadn't seen Alice in seven weeks. She was five thousand miles away, but we had planned for a brief reunion while the helicopter would be serviced for its mandated 100-hour maintenance - which was scheduled in Chile of all places, at that country's only Robinson dealership: Julio's hangar. The very day before the starter failed, Alice had boarded a plane in Washington that would bring her to me. We were to spend a few days together in Valparaiso, while the helicopter would undergo its oil changes and other checkups, at Julio's, which is why we knew who to call when the starter failed. The last thing I needed was engine trouble in the middle of nowhere, five hundred miles from where my girl was just arriving.

I am one straight out of Samuel Johnson's book, because hope does indeed often triumph over experience and that's precisely what old Sam had been referring to: people who divorce and yet try it all over again. Almost half of all marriages in America break up at some point, just as they do in Britain. In Germany the number is forty percent, and in Holland it is one-third. Marriage is an expression of optimism, always and everywhere, ever since people were given a free choice. Other people's divorces do not discourage, nor does one's own. Getting remarried is optimism with a double exclamation point. Eighty percent of all divorced Americans remarry.

***

Faith, hope and love. Isabella was only fifteen, in late April of the year 1466, when in Madrid she was found on her knees, her eyes closed, absorbed in a passionate prayer. She was the young princess of Castile, and a much older man was on his way with an army of three thousand soldiers to arrange the details of their impending marriage. No one had asked Isabella anything; the family was marrying her off. She prayed fervently that the man would be struck by lightning, and if this was too much to ask for, she prayed, would God then please remove her from the land of the living. She wanted a man, gladly even, but she wanted to choose him herself.

Isabella's prayer was answered.[76] Pedro Giron, 43 years old, unmarried but already the father of four children, died on his way to Madrid. Isabella knew by heart the text of the epistle the Bible attributes to the apostle Paul. She had faith in it, she hoped for it, she longed for true love. She finally found it, in the arms of Ferdinand, the young ruler of neighboring Aragon. It became one of the most talked about marriages of the

Renaissance era, in which she had equal rights, and sometimes a little more.

It was no accident, no fluke of history, no surprise. Back to John Simpson of the Oxford dictionary. The first job they gave him to do involved formulating definitions for the word *queen*. He found seven different uses, such as the queen as the ruler of a country, or as the consort of a king, or as an image on a playing card. The queen could also be either a woman or a location that was considered the best in a group or environment, and she could be the prettiest girl wearing a sash at a festival. John mentioned the queen as the one who lays all the eggs for a colony of bees. And also as the most powerful piece on a chessboard.

The chessboard queen. She has everything to do with Queen Isabella. And with Queen Mary of Gelre, with Mary of Scotland, Jacoba of Bavaria, Elizabeth I, Eleanore of Provence and Eleanore of Aquitaine, with Margaret of Parma, the sisters Queen Mary and Queen Anne, and even with Lady Macbeth, not Shakespeare's, but the real one.[77] They were not exceptions, they were often the rule. Ever since the days of Princess Theophano of Byzantium who succeeded her late emperor husband, and of her contemporary the majesty Aedelflaed and her daughter, who ruled the English Midlands - and that's when William the Conqueror had yet to sail across the Channel, Queen Maud's grandfather. Empress Gisela who held what is now Germany under both her thumbs, Petronella of Aragon and her neighbor, Urraca of Leon-Castile, both reigning monarchs: rule, no exception.

Isabella was a contemporary of Martin Luther's. He wrote a bestseller, but not the best-selling book at the time. That distinction was reserved even then for the book of faith, hope and love, the Bible, still the number one best-selling book of all times worldwide today. Luther's was not even number two. The runner-up bestselling book in those days was a publication, written in Latin, entitled *The Book of the Customs of Men and the Duties of Nobles*. It became more popularly known as *The Book of Chess*. Written by James de Cessolis.

He was a Dominican monk, which in and by itself was significant.[78] For by the time his book came off printing presses everywhere around Europe, translated and all, answering a continent-wide demand, the queen was considered the boss of the chessboard. More powerful than the king, more powerful than the bishop. The church of Rome accepted as a given that the social position of women was changing. Even then.

For a thousand years there had been no woman in chess. The game had traveled from India to Persia, and by the time it reached Europe the board featured elephants, horses, chariots, eight soldiers and the shah, for whom the word chess was named. The shah, the king, had one counsellor, the vizier, a position that did not exist in Europe in the late Middle Ages. In the courts of Europe, the king's intimate right hand, the one he listened to, was his wife. The one who shared not only his court, but also his bed.

She held a position that was to be taken seriously, one with which no one else in the court could compete. The existence of a royal bedfellow led to changes on the chessboard. The tusks of elephants became the two tips of a mitre, and so Jumbo became a bishop. The vizier became a queen. Initially moving one diagonal step forward or backward at a time, but she was soon given free rein: the only chess piece that may move unlimitedly in all directions, more influential than the church. Chess was played all over Europe, monk De Cessolis's book became a top bestseller, and meanwhile tall cathedrals were rising up left and right, dedicated to Notre Dame, Our Lady, for Mary was receiving an upgrade as well.[79]

That is why not too many people were surprised when first all those Aedelflaeds, Urracas, Giselas, Eleanores, and then Isabella of Castile, Elizabeth the First, the Marys, Margaret and

Anna, and so on, not only exercised real political and military power, but were recognized and accepted as such by the men of their day. Women began a march toward equality that was slow, but that on balance was and remains unstoppable. There were and always are groups of men who have difficulty dealing with it, but that's tantamount to fighting windmills. Checkmate is their fate, in original Persian *shah mat*. It meant *the king is helpless*.

Chapter 11

The strong women
of Iceland

Optimism that comes with being born a woman

Iceland has a history of strong women. They were no less Viking than the men a thousand years ago, and when Iceland's independence is celebrated every June 17 with a parade, the *fjallkona* leads the way. She is the Lady of the Mountain, the incarnation of both country and nation. Iceland's women were excited when the national airline named a new Boeing for Gudrid Thorbjarnarsdottir.[80] She was the first European woman to set foot on North American soil, just north of Maine, side by side with her husband Thorfinn, in or around the year 1000. Every Icelander knows Gudrid's name.[81] She gave birth to little Snorri Thorfinnsson, the first European baby born on the new continent. To no one's surprise, roughly a millennium later, Iceland became the world's first country to elect a woman president and head of state.[82]

Every year for a century and a half now, they have been celebrating *konadagur*, Women's Day, at the end of February.

The date is related to the return of the sun over the mountains. For the vast majority of Icelanders, this means: over the fjord cliffs, because just about everyone lives along the coast - the interior is largely inhospitable. The strip of habitable fjord land is narrow, fjord mountain flanks often rise steep and perpendicular. For three or four winter months, when there is only a handful of hours of daylight this close to the Arctic Circle, no one sees the actual sun. It lingers too low behind the mountains.

Unless they worked at sea, as most Icelandic men did for centuries. Then they'd often be away from home the entire work week, away from the mountainsides, and they could from their ship see the sun behind the gray clouds. Women and children, however, stayed at home on land, all days, on the narrow coastal strip covered with black sand and gravel because Iceland is also fire land, dotted with active volcanoes.[83] For centuries, being a woman was all about toiling and laboring. On her shoulders rested the responsibility of bringing her usually numerous offspring into the world, keeping them healthy, raising them and delivering them into adulthood safely. In addition to all that, too often the husband did not return home. Death by drowning at sea lurked as a shadow over the shoulders of every Icelandic family until not even that long ago.

She pulled it off, again and again, every generation. She was tough, the boss of the house, mentally independent, and if she did not feel like marrying the father of her child, she simply didn't. Still today, more children are born out of wedlock in Iceland than in most other places in the world, and the law supports the woman. Deadbeat fathers are promptly prosecuted.

The Mountain Woman is however not the only gift from the rocks, not by a long shot. In the weeks before Christmas, Gryla, a cruel mountain ogress who catches naughty children and cooks them into a soup, also makes her appearance. She has thirteen sons, rowdy but generally well-behaved boys who leave small gifts or candy in the shoes of Icelandic children during the thirteen nights leading up to Christmas. But Gryla herself, and her black cat, are not to be trifled with, so you had better mind your manners and don't trigger her attention. That's what her third husband learned to do, a slouch who day and night is lounging around somewhere in the lava fields, but who does not get in her way and is therefore allowed to stay. His two predecessors on the other hand, according to lore, she bit to death and ate.

Gryla is an ogress, but also half elf, a remarkable combination because elves in Iceland are *hildufolk*, small creatures, hidden people. More than half of all Icelandic women believe in their existence. Elves are not like Peter Pan's Tinkerbell. They, too, live in the rocks, and although they are officially gender neutral, it is mainly Icelandic girls who are given elf names at birth: Álfhildur, Álfgerdur, Álfheidur, Álfrún. Elfs are stronger than humans and their machines.

I have lived in Iceland off and on for five years, in the Reykjavik suburb of Kopavogur. Near Álfholsvegur, a road that halfway makes a short detour around a small rock. When the road was constructed a hundred years ago, the rock refused to be pushed aside. Drill bits broke off. And because the country has a special elf expert on hand who in such cases is consulted, the road was routed around the stone at his recommendation. Fifty years later, the street was widened and re-paved. Down with that hill now, said the town. But again the rock did not budge, and this time the road workers refused to touch it any further. The stone hill houses a community of elves, was the collective conclusion. No matter whoever bothers them, they are going to make their life miserable and, worst case scenario, they will come and get them, one way.[84]

The rest of the world smiles and attributes this to the centuries of isolation of a people on a cold island in the middle of the Arctic Ocean. All that Icelanders themselves know is that this is normal fare, par for their course, and no one scoffs at it. I once offered a young local computer programmer a hundred dollars if he'd kick one of those elf stones. He refused, because "who knows, maybe it's true." His wife sighed in horror at the mere thought. Stay away from invisible forces between heaven and earth that we cannot see and yet are here, mothers tell their children. They help, provided you treat them well. And on help, Icelandic women have always counted, in their long, dark winters with all that ice and snow and the ever-present force of gale winds. Without such hope it wouldn't be doable, it would drive them crazy.

***

Icelandic women are second only to Americans at taking the most antidepressants in the world, one in ten of them. That's twice as many as women in France and Germany, and two and a half times as many as Dutch women. But French, Dutch, German and American women commit suicide twice more often than their Icelandic counterparts, and English women are somewhere in between. In all countries, more men end their lives than women, twice as many on average, except in the U.S., where four times as many men commit suicide.[85]

Hope and faith want a little help now and then. That's why people pray or drink. Or they take a pill. It is mostly Icelandic women over 60 who go to the doctor and ask for antidepressants. This is not so much a sign that in the long run they can no longer cope with those long winters, but rather that psychosocial health care in Iceland has a lower threshold. Icelandic women are no more mentally feeble than folks in other countries, quite the contrary. They have a history of never giving up. Their habitat alone commands it. Therefore, in 1615, they were at the forefront when a law dictated that Spanish whalers who came to threaten their livelihoods be put to death. They slashed along together with the men. The law was not officially abolished until 2015, four hundred years later.

Women as a group have often been portrayed worldwide as more pessimistic than men, wrongly so. Recent detailed studies suggest the opposite.[86] Women on average have a longer life expectancy than men, that's one, not because their lives are any less physically demanding. It is simpler that that: on balance they are sunnier. But two, they also have a neurobiological advantage. It takes a serious amount of congenital optimism to carry a pregnancy for three quarters of a year without being in a permanent state of panic as to how that child is eventually going to come into the world. Ask a man to imagine this, and he shudders.

Delivering, having and raising children has always come with worries, especially during the thousands of years of knowing that infant mortality was a regular occurrence. Mothers worldwide, since time immemorial, have passed their stress test with flying colors. Fathers have only over the course of the past century, step by baby step, become more closely involved in the day-to-day upbringing of their brood. Ten thousand years of parenting history is primarily the story of women who, with success and determination, have kept their spirits up.

And what of all the happy women who never had any children? That's what researchers wanted to know, so they went to a convent in Milwaukee.[87] For seventy long and patient years, they studied a group of nearly two hundred nuns who took their vows at about the same time in the same area. Known as the Milwaukee Nuns, they made an ideal test group because their lives after joining the order were almost exact copies of each other. Free of variables: same food, same work, same health care, same environment, same routines. There were only two things that were not similar: their attitude and what they individually expected from life.

Before taking their vows, the nuns were asked to write an essay on how they saw their lives up to that day. Some were cheerful; others were more somber. The cheerful nuns used merry words of gratitude and purpose, such as "eager," "joy," and "happy". The less genial nuns could not think of a single positive word. The best one of them got out of her pen was, "With God's grace, I intend to do my best for my order, for the spread of religion and for my personal sanctification." No enthusiasm, no cheering, no emotion. Her name was Sister Marguerite and she died after a stroke at the age of 59, which fit seamlessly with the overall results of the study.

Of the most positive nuns, ninety percent were still alive at age 85. Of the unhappy nuns, only 34 percent were still breathing at that time. Of the most happy and grateful one-fourth of sisters, more than half were also still alive at age 94. Of the unhappiest ones that number was only 11 percent. On average, the sunniest nuns lived about nine years longer than less happy nuns. And, interesting detail, among those who lived to an advanced age, those who were able to express themselves with the least restraint when in their early twenties they wrote their mini-autobiographies, who found the words to explain exactly what they were so happy and excited about, no one suffered from Alzheimer's disease. That condition occurred exclusively in the category of not-so-happy nuns.

***

Flateyri is a small village on a narrow headland in Iceland's Önundarfjord. One day the butcher there was visited by a farmer who lived across the water. The farmer had to reduce his livestock by order of the government, so he came to have his cow Harpa slaughtered. But Harpa broke loose and ran into the sea.

The water in Icelandic fjords is cold, and the distance to the other side is more than a mile. It took Harpa an hour to cross. On the other shore she was embraced by the farmer's family who had actually not wanted to let her go, and by neighbors who offered to adopt the cow right there and then. After eight months, Harpa gave birth to a healthy calf. She was pregnant when she was about to be slaughtered, and she was the only one who knew it.

Everyone in Iceland is aware of her story from 1987 and the new name she received: *Saeunn*, wave on the sea. Mothers give their children the booklet *Sundkyrin Saeunn* to read, Saeunn the swimming cow. And every year toward the end of summer, men and women swim across the fjord, the Saeunn swimming race. The cow lived to last another six happy years. She rests on the beach under a burial hill of small boulders that have come rolling in from the ocean. She is considered a symbol of all that is good, stubborn and optimistic about the nation of Iceland.

Chapter 12

Setting clocks at sea

When optimism causes major harm

It's a remarkable phenomenon, one we don't usually dwell on, but throughout all the ages, adversity has been a greater inspiration for optimism than when things went according to plan. Inspiration, as in: misery triggering a redoubled effort to prevent it from happening again. When things go wrong, the glass on this book's front cover pops up: is it half full or half empty. Everyone recognizes a tendency, when faced with a setback, of dejection, of finding yourself down in the dumps, from disappointment, sadness, discouragement. But staying there forever? Nah.

That's now how we, creatures with that big brain, are built. We are not called *sapiens*, wise thinkers, for nothing. Thinking leads to associating, one thought prompting the next. And so, a century and a half ago, someone sat twiddling with a piece of wire, probably lost in thought, thinking about something completely unrelated, until he suddenly realized he had made a little binder: the birth of the paper clip.[88]

Or that time during World War I when cotton was in short supply. Someone somewhere had seen that a certain wood pulp, like the stuff that Garrett Schenck's Millinocket plant produced, could be made into a type of paper with an unusually high absorption capacity. Before long the product landed on the battlefields, as an emergency bandage for wounded soldiers, as a sanitary pad for Red Cross nurses and as a filter in gas masks. Now everyone knows it as Kleenex.[89]

This was in response to a pressing and acute problem, but even smaller irritations can have major consequences. Georges de Mestral was walking his dog in the Swiss Alps one morning when he noticed that Milka's coat was covered in burrs, and so were his own pant legs. He removed them, took one home, put it under a microscope and saw that nature had outfitted the thingy with hundreds of tiny hooks. They attached themselves to anything they perceived as a loop. Georges invented Velcro.[90] Ten years later, Neil Armstrong and Buzz Aldrin walked on the moon with Velcro under their shoes. They used it to stick their footwear to a special panel on the wall once they returned to the command capsule so that shoes wouldn't bother the astronauts by floating around.

But all these examples pale into insignificance when compared to one of the classic examples of adversity that inspires. Once more we go briefly back to the man of the dictionary. For not included in John Simpson's definitions of *queen* was the meaning of *queen of heaven and earth*, a Roman Catholic title reserved for the Virgin Mary, for Notre Dame. In Portuguese, she is named Madre de Deus, the mother of God.

It was the name the Portuguese gave in 1589 to their newest and largest cargo ship, around the end of the Renaissance. She was deployed on the southern trade route to and from the Far East. Returning on her second voyage, the Madre de Deus ran straight into an English fleet. The crew was overpowered and everything on board was confiscated. Everything, that was gold, silver coins, pearls, diamonds, amber, carpets and lots of spices: two hundred tons of pepper, cloves, cinnamon and nutmeg. The destination was Lisbon, but it all ended up in London. The street value of Madre de Deus's cargo was more than half the entire English treasury.[91]

Everyone knew how this could have happened. The Portuguese captain had lost his way. No one at sea had any idea of longitudes, therefore all a sailor could do was guess by the sun, moon and stars, without any precision, and only if and when the sky was not overcast. In London, people cheered and partied, but that was premature. About a hundred years later, in 1707, four English warships ran aground at the Scilly Isles - those rocks eternally bombarded by the ocean with that abandon we discussed earlier. Fifteen hundred sailors drowned, including the fleet admiral.

The story goes that the day before, a sailor had warned the admiral that, according to his amateur calculation, they were off course, but the boss considered him insubordinate in an attempt to cause panic, which was a serious offense on board. The sailor was hung from the tallest mast, but it turned out he was right, and the shipwreck still ranks as one of the worst in English naval history. It offered yet another urgent incentive for taking the challenge of solving this particular navigational problem seriously. The English government offered cash prizes, which helped. The promise of rewards does for inventors what jackpots do for lottery participants: it acutely fuels their optimism.

Latitudes had been known for some time. After Columbus persuaded Queen Isabella and her husband in 1492 to cover the expense of his first expedition across the Atlantic, he initially sailed down the coast to the Canary Islands, and from there he headed west across the ocean. Columbus thought the wind blew him in more or less a straight line toward Asia, along a single latitude. He was wrong by four degrees, veered three hundred miles off course, but made landfall anyway, although not in Asia. All 180 latitudes are parallel to each other, each at a distance of some seventy miles. Sailing from east to west and back had been possible for a long time, because the position of the sun, moon and stars helped seamen do so.

But for sailing between north and south they were of no help, and the trade shipping lanes from east to west and back first ran north-south along the full length of Africa, and vice versa. Longitudes have no parallels, their distance to the next one is nowhere the same. At the north and south poles there is zero separation between them, but at the equator the gap is as wide as it is between two latitudes. When the Madre de Deus sailed into a trap, primitive compasses existed in China, and by the time the English fleet went down, experiments were being made with a sextant. But both were useless anyway if sailors didn't know what longitude they were at or near. They could only figure that out if they knew what time it was.

This was the trick that British carpenter John Harrison came up with. He spent years working on inventing a wooden clock that would withstand sailing. The clock had to be able to tolerate swells, tilt, water, and salt, and moreover it could not run ahead or behind by more than three seconds. It was a challenge. No clock had ever had to meet those requirements before. Finally, after six years, Harrison succeeded. More and more metal parts were added, and finally in 1736 he demonstrated it for astronomer Edward Halley, of comet fame, who arranged for it to be tested at sea. The contraption, as an appropriate tribute to Portugal and Madre de Deus, was sailed back and forth from London to Lisbon. It worked.

Now suddenly every ship could determine longitude by having two clocks on board. One showed the time of the home port, and the other was synchronized each day with the location at sea, which was fairly easy to determine at noon, when the sun reached its apex. Each hour of time difference meant that fifteen degrees of longitude had been traveled: 360

degrees divided by 24 hours. Instantly, sailing became much safer, and carpenter John Harrison won the jackpot.

***

Not a day too soon, for commercial shipping had long been a vital part of the European economies. The exploration for safer and shorter routes was in full swing, with increasing success. Within a period of less than three decades, Christopher Columbus landed off the coast of the Americas, Vasco da Gama rounded the Cape of Good Hope, and Ferdinand Magellan discovered a way to round the tip of South America. All this transpired around the beginning of the sixteenth century, in part because explorers could now read each other's travel accounts in book form.

Something was bubbling in Europe, something was changing. Not the pace of motion, which would remain unchanged for another three centuries. But people could read and be read, they could report on the latest discoveries, on new insights and ideas, and on stories travelers came home with. Knowledge invites comparing, and leads to learning that there is more beyond the horizon than had previously been assumed. Competition between cities, city-states and larger states changed. With often lasting consequences. Europe's financial and economic center of gravity shifted from the Mediterranean to the north.

All this went hand in hand with the spirit of the times, the departure from the Middle Ages. The continent declared itself reborn, resurrected from what was considered the beauty and wisdom of long-ago classical antiquity. The Renaissance produced fine arts, in Florence, Pisa, Rome, and in Venice which became a center of printing. But it also produced corrupt popes and civic leaders, and arrogance. Sixteen-year-old Michelangelo Buonarroti was already pompous and self-absorbed at that young an age to such a degree that he took it out on an older fellow student. In response, the angered guy punched him in the face, leaving the future sculptor of David and painter of the Sistine Chapel ceiling with a deformed nose for the rest of his life.[92] No one was surprised; manners during the seemingly peaceful Renaissance were often rough and raw.

These were energetic times on the continent, but at the same time they were a challenge for many. There had always been tensions and armed conflicts between England and France, between Spain and Portugal, between Iberia and the Moors, between Genoa, Rome or Venice among themselves and with the Ottoman sultan, with constantly changing alliances, century after century. But the mass production of bronze led to a mass production of cannons. Stronger weapons led to bloodier battle scenes. Cities and fortresses that had been impregnable for centuries now grew vulnerable. The word spread, and suddenly European kings, dukes and cardinals had options available, choices.

They could fight if they managed to raise enough soldiers, or they could make one great empire out of two smaller ones through marriage. Because each of those options required finances, they increasingly leaned on bankers. It made Jakob Fugger in Augsburg the world's first billionaire; for a time he had his fingers in just about every alliance and military confrontation.[93] He could choose any which way he wanted, for nowhere else in the world was the landscape of power and politics so fragmented as in Europe.

But also: nowhere else did this prompt such an urge to do business, to make money and to constantly seek those shorter and more efficient shipping lanes.[94] It explains the synchronism between the trio of Columbus, Da Gama and Magellan and all the explorers who came after them. But it also illustrates why the continent was so bustling, and why happy faces could be seen more and more frequently in more and more places. Trade always leads to a better quality of life, each time new products become available that make the day more comfortable. While the boundaries of the world as people thought they knew it were pushed farther away, as new shores were being discovered all the time, optimism was king, almost everywhere.

Optimism and confidence go hand in hand. Trade invites investment, and investors keep their money in their pockets until they grow confident that a positive outcome is likely. Super-sized banks were created in Portugal, Spain, Florence, Germany, Austria and Hungary, owned and managed by a handful of super-rich bankers. They wouldn't invest in an ocean expedition or a military campaign without a well-founded expectation of a decent return. Once they did, it fostered close relationships between creditor and debtor, trust between banker and customer, who was typically a wealthy merchant, a ruler, someone with soldiers on hand.

Paper contracts emerged, with the parties knowing full well that they had to stick to them. Not that things never went wrong, or that there was never anyone who proved unreliable after the fact - that happened time and again. But by trial and error, a climate developed of mutual trust in the world of supply and demand for funding. And as each conflict between larger or smaller nations produced not only a winner, but also a loser, the motivation to invent more modern forms of return grew as well.

Buying something and selling it for a higher price. Among all mammals, this occurs only among humans.[95] With mixed results, good and bad, winners and losers, but on balance trade became the all-important driver of progress, growth and prosperity. The law of relative cost advantages reigned supreme: the East preferred to sell silk, carpets and expensive spices to Europe rather than import its linen and cotton. It had plenty of textiles of its own. In exchange, they preferred cash, or free labor. Therefore, increasingly, one European ship after another on its way east interrupted its journey along the coast of Africa and robbed entire communities of their people. Men, women and children were handcuffed and forcibly loaded. Slaves became a currency for silk and spices, the kind of cargo that Portugal's proud new barge Madre de Deus carried.

It contributed greatly to the optimistic worldview of merchants west and east. But it came at an immense price, for it contributed even more so to pessimism and despair along the beaches of Africa. The slave trade became the single greatest stain on the history of optimism - the totally avoidable cause of other people's pain and pessimism.

Chapter 13

The 20th century was the worst and the best

Optimist for a penny

The internet, email, DVDs, iPhones, text messaging, flat TV screens, MRI scanners, Google, the International Space Station, hybrid cars, drones, Dolly the cloned sheep, GPS, Facebook, laptop computers, Nintendo, DNA tests, microprocessors, Tik-Tok, digital cameras, bitcoin, electric cars, Whatsapp, LED light bulbs, Amazon.com, the birth control patch, PlayStation, wifi, Netflix, online banking, Elmo. Things that have become commonplace within a span of just three decades, since 1990. In that year, Italian Toto Cotugno won the Eurovision Song Contest. Toto who?

Things that became common in the forty years preceding 1990: credit cards, robots, transistor radios, hovercrafts, space travel, nuclear power, satellites, video, desktop computers, pacemakers, lasers, the computer mouse, bar codes, in-vitro fertilization, ATMs, supermarkets, mopeds, color TV, cash register scanners, Barbie, the pill, hula hoop, power steering, the hydrogen bomb, hairspray, McDonalds, cassette tapes, calculators, open-heart surgery, vaccinations against mumps and measles, Abba, the floppy disk, disposable lighters, the walkman, weather radar, prozac. In 1950, there was no song festival and no Beatles.

Yearning for the good old days usually dissipates once we start counting everything that didn't exist back then. Much less if we go back yet another half century further, to the year 1900. There was no airplane, bra, zipper, radio, television, radar, plastic, cinemas, a sewage system in Los Angeles, insulin, refrigerator, breast or uterine cancer testing, nylons, freezer, antibiotics, kidney dialysis, velcro, bus transportation, air conditioning, neon, the teddy bear, highways for automobiles, vacuum cleaners, Amelia Earhart, washing machines, gramophone records, tea bags, central heating, tractors, lights in every room of the home, windshield wipers, cornflakes, tanks, crossword puzzles, toasters, band-aids, traffic lights, gas stations, not even a zeppelin yet.

Just about everything we know and can do today originated within a four-generation time frame. During that same period, diphtheria, tetanus, polio, smallpox, tuberculosis, measles, mumps, rubella, foot-and-mouth disease, streptococcal and staphylococcal infections, syphilis, gonorrhea, herpes and malaria were brought under control. AIDS is no longer the threat it was just forty years ago. Thirty months after the Covid outbreak, five billion people worldwide had been vaccinated. One hundred years earlier, when the Spanish flu broke out in Kansas, spreading around the world as infectiously and deadly as Covid, no one was vaccinated. The first vaccination against influenza took place in 1946.[96]

One hundred years ago, barely two billion people lived in our world. Four generations later, that number had quadrupled. Then, the average life expectancy for men was 46 years, for women 48. Now it is 75 and 80 years respectively, not counting Covid's short-term effects. And those are the numbers that apply to the United States. In Western Europe, they are a fraction higher still: 80 years for English men, 83 for women, as is also the case in Holland. German men on average make it to their 79th birthday, women to 85, just like in France.[97]

All these facts, numbers, things, possibilities, people, improvements, accelerations and expansions since 1900 are on the balance sheet of a period of time that also included two world wars, two pandemics, a global economic depression, a bunch of recessions, wars in Asia and Africa, dictatorships in Eastern Europe, South America, China and a handful of neighboring countries, overt racism in America and South Africa, horrific mutilations of young women in the Middle East, a 40-year cold war and a nuclear arms race. What does that tell us?

Nothing, they are statistics. People have not been quartered, broken on the wheel or beheaded in a long time. Ears, noses and genitals are no longer publicly cut off by order of the courts. But the state of Arizona not so long ago, in 1992, executed a German bank robber in a gas chamber for stabbing someone to death with a letter opener that he picked up during the robbery. And Lincoln's killers were not the last to hang from the gallows. It also happened to the murderer of an elderly couple in Delaware in 1996. Public executions are no longer carried out in Mississippi, but since the year 2000, in eight cases young men have been found dead, hanging from a tree branch, and each had a dark skin.[98] No trace of the perpetrators, but evidently lynching is still not a thing of the past.

In short, if there is no more breaking on the wheel, but there's still gassing and hanging, who can say with certainty that there will never be another quartering? Something or someone may be on a right track, but by itself that doesn't predict the future. Suppose you are standing at a window halfway up a skyscraper, and someone comes falling off the roof. If you were to ask him in that split second whether he is still breathing, all the man could say with certainty is: so far so good. Bertrand Russell came up with another example, that of the turkey that, on the day before Thanksgiving, notes with satisfaction that the farmer has been coming to feed him every morning, already for 364 days now. As far as the turkey is concerned, the future looks bright.[99]

In India, rapists still go free. In China, you better not be an Uyghur. In Mexico, drug cartels show each other who's boss by dangling a dozen or so men and women from an overpass after first having tortured them to death. Those who live in a country that borders Russia can expect an invasion at any time. And by the way: no one knows exactly how many pieces of plastic are floating in the oceans, but experts from Earth Day, Oxford University and the Ocean Cleanup project roughly agree that it's over five trillion pieces of trash. That's a 5 with 12 zeros. A new load of plastic equivalent to the content of two garbage trucks is added every minute. A quarter of humanity lives within thirty miles of a seashore, that's why.[100] The main culprits are in Asia because that's where the most people live. Eighty percent of all ocean plastic comes out of Asian rivers.[101]

Eight billion people, together we are making the air worse, the soil dirtier, the earth warmer and we cause sea levels to rise. I readily confess my part. My three months in a helicopter around North and South America alone, over three hundred flight hours, burned almost five thousand gallons of fuel. That didn't leave the world's air any healthier.

Everyone promises to do better. In the same three decades that gave the world all those wonderful things at the top of this chapter began, two major international agreements were negotiated, in Kyoto and Paris, to end pollution. There is little doubt about the good will of the vast majority of the signatories. But again: what does this say? In and by itself, nothing. Tomorrow's good will can become unwillingness the day after. The only guarantee that ten thousand years of creative thinking has produced is that absolutely nothing can be guaranteed.

And yet.

***

People are relentlessly optimistic, despite being surrounded by stubborn facts that almost seem to implore them to abandon all hope. Wishful thinking? Who knows, but there is no arguing with success. All the woes and heartbreak during the era that spanned the past four generations notwithstanding, in the end the world has become a much better place for very many people.

In part, this is because of our unspoken but intuitive doubt about the inevitability of such woes. Were they really, absolutely, one hundred percent unavoidable? Because if the answer is, "Maybe not," as we have assumed a few times before, then did that orgy of violence during the first half of the previous century have an element of bad luck? Do historians look back on it, say, two centuries from now and decide that it was mainly a matter of stress and agitation spiraling out of control?

Yes, says Mathew White, a librarian by profession. Like blind telephone hacker Joe Engressia did, he hails from Richmond, Virginia. He read everything about wars he could get his hands on in the library. Not just wars from the last century, but battles and conflicts of all times. He wrote a book about the hundred deadliest conflicts since the second Persian War, which took place in the year 480 BC.[102] White made some waves because Harvard's optimism psychologist Pinker became impressed by his knowledge, and began quoting him.

A frequently asked question in the year 1999, as the millennium drew to a close, sought to know who had been the most important person of the 20th century. Mathew White responded. He did not choose Einstein, the Wright brothers, Hitler, Hemingway, Madame Curie, Churchill or Mother Theresa. He chose Gavrilo Prinzip.

Prinzip was the nineteen-year-old rebellious student in Sarajevo who in 1914, to his own surprise, after an earlier failed assassination attempt, saw his target pass by once more, in an open car that came to a stop right in front of him. "Here," White said, "is a man who single-handedly sets off a chain reaction, which ultimately leads to the death of 80 million people. With just a couple of bullets, this terrorist starts the First World War which destroys four monarchies, leading to a power vacuum filled by the Communists in Russia and the Nazis in Germany who then fight it out in a Second World War."[103]

Exaggerated? At the time, virtually everybody was dumbfounded that the assassination of a dignitary in Sarajevo could have served as a fuse for such an uncontrolled sequence of events. Agitated hotheads going overboard in the Balkans, that wasn't really unique. Just six years earlier, a book by the title *The Great Illusion* had been a bestseller on the continent, selling a million copies in 22 languages. In it, journalist Norman Angell argued that no one in Europe would ever think of starting another war, because the economic consequences would be insurmountably disastrous. There was simply no rationale that any reasonable person could conjure up as to why the continent should ignite. Even Kaiser Wilhelm read the book, reportedly agreeing with it.[104]

What if? History is a hodgepodge of freak hits and misses, we noted earlier. What if, on May 17, 1916, senator Harding had not mailed that letter to his lover next door, caving to her demand that he not run for president that year? The war had been going on for almost two years by then, but America was not yet involved. Harding was widely seen as the most popular politician in the country, and the contest over who would occupy the White House next seemed his to lose. But he cleared the way for the incumbent occupant, just-married Woodrow Wilson who was re-elected.

America was sucked into the war within a matter of months, Germany lost, Wilson went to Paris and proved himself the worst possible peace negotiator. The Versailles Treaty radicalized Germany and caused such a devastating inflation that a streetcar ticket in Berlin that in 1914 a passenger would have paid 1 D-mark for, cost them 15 million marks in 1922.[105] Harding vehemently disagreed with what Wilson stood for in just about every respect, and when he decided to run for president in 1920 after all, he was overwhelmingly elected. But by then it was too late to prevent the escalations that reignited Europe.

What if? What if Gavrilo Prinzip hadn't done this, what if Warren Harding hadn't done that? The world will never know, but if there's one thing people have learned over the course of millennia, it is that nothing is forever inevitable. That is why there's always a Florence Nightingale somewhere who is going to do something about it. Twelfth-century Eleanore of Aquitaine was one of them.[106] She was adamant that the subordination of women to men had to end, and she divorced first the French, then the English king and continued to rule without them. Martin Luther was another. Popes and bishops who promised God's forgiveness of all sins in exchange for bribes, he was going to do something about that. Dorothea Dix from Hampden, Maine was one, fighting to establish the rights of the mentally ill[107]. Ernest Hemingway who went to Spain to fight Franco's fascists. Nelson Mandela who was going to end a major injustice.

In the first half of the 20th century, the world ran amok. A truly, tragic bad break, says the author of the book about the hundred worst wars, with grotesquely dramatic consequences. It could have been avoided if Archduke Franz Ferdinand's chauffeur had not turned right. Saying such things out loud is like swearing in the temple for those whose pain is still too fresh. But something in all of us recognizes elements of Mathew White's argument. Humanity has never given up. And at the end of the day perhaps the strongest evidence of this is the staggering amount of good the twentieth century has produced.

***

The idea of attempting to set a record by helicopter arose in March 2006 during a flight between Florida and Maryland. I asked pilot Stephan for his opinion. Did he think it could be done, with this small helicopter, first flying to Alaska, then down to Panama, across the canal there, into South America until we reached the bottom end of Patagonia? And then from there back up again, once more crossing the Panama Canal, until we were back in Maryland? "I mean, does it matter to the helicopter where she flies?" I asked. Stephan thought about it, then agreed, "No, it doesn't, and yes, this should be doable." A helicopter only cares about chopping air with the rotor blades, about making wind that creates lift. Which air, and where, she couldn't care less.

We made a stop along the way in Georgia, at Savannah's airport. You land where the control tower says your parking spot is, usually coming in on a final descent to where those large numbers on the runway are painted, and from there you hover at a few feet above the ground towards the designated spot. Next a fuel truck arrives, halts in front of the helicopter, and fills both fuel tanks. Payment takes place inside the office of what is generally known as the FBO, the fixed-base operator. So I opened the door to that office, and on the threshold I noticed a penny on the floor right in front of me. I picked it up and saw that it was not a regular dollar cent. It was *Un centesimo de Balboa*, it said, and along the edge it read, *Republica de Panama*.

What are the odds of finding a Panamanian cent somewhere, anywhere, ten minutes after debating amongst ourselves crossing the Panama Canal not once, but twice? Not that big, I thought. Not bigger or smaller than winning the jackpot using a fortune cookie. I decided right there and then to make the odyssey. After all, sometimes a penny is all that optimism needs.

Chapter 14

The day Maine's Roswell saved the world

The optimism of lessons learned

Mount Desert Island is northeastern Maine's largest island, green, mountainous, water, streams, lakes and coves everywhere. The trees on its shores were cut down long ago. The Rockefellers used to come here in the summers, and the Roosevelts. They built homes from the lumber that Samuel Gilpatrick's sawmill cut for them. Sam himself lived on what today is still called Gilpatrick Cove, on land he had cleared with his own hands. Once, way back when, they had come to Maine from Scotland via Ireland, the Gilpatricks. They helped first George Washington chase the English out of the country, and when the redcoats returned in 1812 and refused to leave Maine, there was not a single Gilpatrick who wouldn't join the militia to kick their British butts.

They now rest at Brookside Cemetery in Northeast Harbor. Without the K. Walter Gilpatrick, a Wall Street lawyer, decided to drop the K and spell his name Gilpatric, and therefore his four children were also named that way. Roswell was the oldest, born in 1906, his summers spent playing in Maine with his childhood friend Nelson Rockefeller who was born around the corner, in Bar Harbor. Now and then I run an unscientific survey, and I ask people if they know who Ros Gilpatric was. Crickets, without exception.

On October 22, 1962, Ros Gilpatric saved the world. Nothing more, nothing less.

When I ask people about Ros's buddy, everyone nods and knows his name. He was Robert McNamara, secretary of defense during the Kennedy and Johnson administrations. One day I sat down and had lunch with him: "Hi, I am Bob." He had brought a table companion, Madelin. Rumor had it that he did so in order to behave better. Bob by himself could be insufferable, always and forever convinced he was right, a problem exacerbated by the reality that he often was.

"Stop the projector." He was once in a meeting that lasted eight hours, in Hawaii. That was where the military headquarters was located that oversaw the war in Vietnam. McNamara was everybody's boss there, so they promptly did as he said. "This slide, number 869, contradicts slide 11." The generals checked, and sure enough, the secretary was right. "Everyone was impressed," David Halberstam later wrote in *The Best and the Brightest*, "and many a little frightened."[108] Such a mastery of data, numbers and facts made people around him nervous. There was a time when no one in his presence dared broach the subject of Vietnam. Halfway through the word, "Viet...," his stare had already killed you.[109]

We sat at a round table, "Hi, I'm Bob," he said a second time, indicating he was in a talkative mood. I sat at his left side, Madelin at his other. McNamara was a widower by this time, so no one thought there was anything funny about him bringing someone along for company. As for her, the same thing. She was divorced, since quite some time ago, from the man McNamara described to me as "my right-hand man." Madelin Thayer had been Ros Gilpatric's third wife; two more wives would follow after her, but none of those successors were the reason for the divorce. That was Jackie Kennedy. McNamara's right-hand man had an affair with the wife of their boss.

Roswell Gilpatric was deputy defense secretary. Normally, the secretary selects his own deputy, but in this case the president himself had made the choice. McNamara came from the business world, from Dearborn, Michigan where he was the CEO of the Ford automobile company, with no experience in political Washington. But he was considered a genius, unusually forceful and decisive, a born manager. Gilpatric was something of a prodigy too, himself a successful lawyer at an early age. Ros's mom had been a friend of Frances Perkins from Newcastle, Maine, who was America's first female cabinet minister during the Franklin Roosevelt administration, and after Roosevelt's death his successor Harry Truman had appointed Ros undersecretary of the Air Force. Kennedy expected that McNamara and Gilpatric, a life-long Republican, would complement each other well.

Sure enough, they clicked; they became close friends. So when the Cuban missile crisis erupted in October 1962, it was Bob and Ros who were sitting side by side at Kennedy's table for two weeks in a feverish effort to prevent a nuclear war. The Soviet Union had been stationing nuclear missiles in Cuba, and the Pentagon's spy planes had detected it. The discovery was kept secret for the time being, and now the trick was how to prevent worse from happening. That didn't come easy. The president had gathered a special team around him for the occasion, and they included a few hawks who urged him to bomb the Russian positions right away, before the missiles would become operational.

Kennedy wasn't sure this was a good idea. It seemed better to try to verbally scare off his counterpart Khrushchev in Moscow first, without immediately waking sleeping dogs at home. He gave the job to Gilpatric, usually a man of few words. Ros scheduled a public speaking arrangement somewhere, and there he warned the Russians about the disastrous boomerang consequences of a nuclear attack, for the Russians themselves. Kennedy had guessed correctly, in his own country no one paid attention to a deputy secretary, but Khrushchev kept a close eye on what words came out of the Pentagon. He responded by saying that he did not want to be treated like a small child, and did not signal that he had taken the indirect message to heart.[110]

This prompted the hawks to argue for bombing even stronger. "Do you remember, Madelin," McNamara said over our lunch, "how enormous that pressure was on us?" Madelin nodded. Back then she was still married to Ros, and she remembered those days all too well. She had sensed there was something going on between her husband and the president's wife, and a few years later she would see it confirmed in black and white. That was after someone had stolen a stack of letters from Gilpatric's safe that next ended up at an auction house. They were Jackie Kennedy's letters to "Dearest Ros," thanking him for stolen hours together while the president was off traveling for a few days.[111] "Imagine," Bob said of the peer pressure in 1962, "if we had done that," bombing Cuba preemptively.

In that strange circumstance of a world on the brink of an all-destroying nuclear war, with a president who was urgently seeking advice from his aides, including the man I was now breaking bread with, plus the man who in his spare time was also pleasuring the First Lady - in that setting Kennedy had to choose. His security adviser Bundy and his Secretary of State Rusk were telling him he had only one choice, and that was to attack, right now. His Secretary of Defense McNamara was fiercely opposed to that and instead recommended a blockade of Cuba, at sea, which was less aggressive and possibly much more effective. Unbeknownst to the others, Kennedy had listening devices installed in the room. The tape recorder listened in and documented an uneasy silence, that 22nd of October.

It was Ros Gilpatric who then pushed history into the right direction. He broke the silence in the room, and said, forcefully, "Essentially, Mr. President, this is a choice between limited action and unlimited action, and most of us think it is better to start with limited action."[112] And that was what the president decided to do. Muscles were flexed, but there was no fighting. Diplomatic negotiations ensued, and eventually Cuba's nuclear weapons disappeared.

Nevertheless, McNamara said some thirty years later, "Imagine if we had done that," such a pre-emptive strike urged by not the least among Kennedy's advisers. It was the reason for our lunch conversation. He had recently visited Moscow, and I asked him about it. Government delegations from the U.S., the Soviet Union and Cuba had convened to review their 1962 experiences together. They were the decision makers of that time, men who were in charge when the missile crisis occurred. Michael Gorbachev had initiated the meeting in the name of perestroika and glasnost, and President Bush senior had wholeheartedly approved it.

McNamara recounted how at that Moscow meeting everyone was shocked when Soviet archives were produced. They revealed what in 1962 no one in the White House knew. The Kremlin had secretly given the go-ahead for the local Russian commander in Cuba to use tactical nuclear weapons as he saw fit if America attacked first. He did not need to seek permission in Moscow for doing so. "Can you imagine what that would have meant?" said McNamara now. He was still outraged by so much nonchalance.[113] "You don't leave the responsibility for starting a nuclear war in the hands of an officer in the field."

The world had squeezed through an even narrower eye of the needle than was already suspected at the time.

Coincidence, or the result of careful policy? There exists much documentation about the top-secret deliberations inside the White House walls from those days, in addition to the tape recordings. In that contemporaneous historiography, McNamara, Gilpatric, the president and his brother Robert come out favorably. It suggests that diligence won the day. But meanwhile, Gilpatric and McNamara's spy flights over Cuba continued, and one of those planes was shot down. It could easily have been the fatal spark.

Except that it wasn't. Back to Mathew White, the author of the book on history's 100 worst wars, the man who in late 1999, looking back on the 20th century, claimed that the two world wars had not been inevitable. "No more inevitable than, say, a war between NATO and the Warsaw Pact."[114] That war almost came. But not quite. The world was on a knife-edge, and the knife tipped the right way. A nuclear war was avoided. Because at a crucial moment, the U.S. president trusted the recommendation of a man from Maine who was secretly making out with Mrs Kennedy, and whom he could and did therefore privately not trust at all.

***

Something in all of us intuitively knows that shit happens, sometimes inevitably, like weather events, volcanic eruptions or an occasional epidemic, but most of it is essentially avoidable. The fact that avoidable woes nonetheless afflict the world does not make the vast majority of people naturally pessimistic. On the contrary, for although our actions often seem to suggest that we rarely learn from mistakes made - in reality, as a species we all learn very well. Few generations make the same mistakes that the previous ones made. Let me give you the example of the city of San Francisco.

In the spring of 1906, Maarten and Jan Bekius decided to build a storage building in San Francisco, constructed of reinforced concrete. They were the owners of a moving company. Maarten had turned the *u* in Bekius upside down into an *n* because Americans could pronounce it better, and he was now spelling his own name Martin, while Jan became John. Their parents Sjoerd and Tietje had emigrated from Hallum, the Netherlands, to Michigan at the end of the 19th century, taking their 13 children with them. The brothers moved on to the West Coast because big cities were growing there, Los Angeles, West Hollywood, Sacramento, Seattle, San Francisco. Soon Bekins became an in-demand moving company.

Building with concrete was not popular in San Francisco. High-rise concrete buildings had only recently begun to appear, in Chicago and New York, but most people thought they looked unappealing. Moreover, California's construction unions were vehemently against it. Houses and stores were either made of timber, usually from the towering redwoods, or they were made of brick. In California the building industry was employing thousands of carpenters and masons. Their unions firmly opposed using concrete in construction.

Martin and John paid no attention to any of this and commissioned a concrete specialist to build a six-story storage building on the outskirts of town.[115] They had an optimistic reason. They felt confident that at the beginning of the new century, with America on a growth spur, their own business would grow just as fast. Therefore, they needed storage space. Concrete was fireproof, which was important when you were storing other people's possessions.

On Wednesday, April 18, a massive earthquake, 7.9 on the Richter scale, hit San Francisco. Houses, stores and commercial buildings collapsed, and fires broke out everywhere. What was made of wood turned to ash. More than three thousand people lost their lives, and three-quarters of all residents became homeless. Only two buildings remained standing. One was San Francisco's Mint Building, constructed of granite. The other was the Bekins warehouse. It had advanced to only two stories, but both were unaffected. The contractor promptly proceeded to finish the building, and within a few years one concrete structure after another rose from the ground, not only in San Francisco, but throughout California and far beyond.

More than a hundred years later, Bekins is now one of America's five largest movers, under contract with the Pentagon since the days when McNamara and Gilpatric were running the place to move military families when a permanent change of station calls for relocation, with three hundred storage centers, two thousand moving vans and five thousand drivers. Bekins was the first to offer storage for people who were not moving, but whose attic or shed was becoming too small and who could not part with their belongings. Today, the United States has more than 50,000 such locations, all modeled after Bekins. The brothers were not just optimistic. They foresaw a trend.

* * *

By the time I sat down to talk to him about the Cuba crisis, Robert McNamara had collected himself again. That was different from the day before. Then, journalist Stanley Karnow and I sat across from him, listening to his success stories about his time as president of the World Bank. Stanley had just won the Pulitzer Prize with a book on America and the Philippines, but he was better known for his reports from and about Vietnam. McNamara was confident about the success of his contribution to fighting world poverty, and he periodically underscored it by saying, "You can take that to the bank."

Karnow had heard this more than once. He interrupted the man he remembered primarily as the defense secretary in charge of the Vietnam War. "You used to say those same words, Bob, when you assured us once again that everything in Vietnam was going in the right direction. 'You can take it to the bank.' And it was a lie. Now why should we believe you're right this time?"

Stanley Karnow knew what he was talking about. His book on the history of Vietnam had aired twice on television as a 13-part series, and he could recite from memory the numbers: nearly 3 million American drafted men sent to Indo China, 150,000 wounded, 58,000 killed, 1 trillion dollars in wasted money[116], a never clarified number of Vietnamese dead. It had been mostly McNamara's war, geared up shortly after reason had prevailed around Cuba. It had sharply divided America and the world; McNamara's own children openly protested against their father. But nothing led him to acknowledge that he regretted the mistakes he had made.

Until now. Robert McNamara suddenly broke down in tears. "What do you want me to say? That I was wrong?" Karnow and I didn't quite know what to make of this sudden emotion and both said nothing. "I was wrong. My God, I was wrong! I'm sorry."

As a group, our species is good at learning; few generations repeat previous generations' errors. Except when it comes to Vietnam. The second half of the last century was one of proxy wars, Korea, Vietnam, Central America, Syria, Lebanon, Angola, Afghanistan. Wars between local opponents, but in reality superpowers fighting each other without openly engaging in one-on-one battles, usually the United States and the Soviet Union. That motivation disappeared with the fall of the Berlin Wall, and suddenly in 1990 both camps fought pretty much side by side in Iraq, after Saddam Hussein had invaded Kuwait.

But old habits don't get ditched easily. America was attacked by al-Qaeda, terrorists who had a home base in Afghanistan, and so it invaded that harsh and hostile terrain, staying and fighting there for twenty years. It invaded Iraq again in 2003 and stayed for eight years. In 2014, it decided to participate in actions in Syria, and at the time I write these words, eight years later, that status quo remains unchanged. It is one thing to find yourself in the role of the world's policeman, since it comes with the territory of being the world's only remaining super-power. But entering battlefields with an attitude as if nothing has been learned from the mistakes of Robert McNamara and his successors, that is a study in avoidability, to say the least.

Chapter 15

The girl who predicted a tsunami

Optimism instilled by underdogs

Tilly Smith from England was ten when her parents took her to Thailand for a Christmas vacation. On the morning of December 26, 2004, they made a beach walk together, and what caught Tilly's eye were the sizzling bubbles in the water. Two weeks earlier, in geography class at school, she had learned how to tell if a tsunami was coming. Bubbles like these were one of the symptoms, as well as ocean water not retreating but creeping farther and farther up the beach.

She was alarmed by what she saw; her mom didn't believe her, but her father did. As he alerted someone at the hotel, a Japanese guest overheard the word *tsunami* and mentioned that an earthquake had hit Sumatra that morning. All tourists were rushed off the beach. The tsunami arrived twenty minutes later and caused the deaths of five thousand Thai people, but no one's on Tilly Smith's beach. She saved the lives of a hundred beach tourists.[117]

The world is not remotely always a happy place. Every six seconds somewhere a child like Tilly dies before turning fifteen, fourteen thousand children every day. Every minute, twenty fathers and mothers stand somewhere mourning by a grave. Those are sobering figures, indicating, among too many other sad facts, that we are still too far removed from finding an adequate answer to leukemia and other childhood cancers, not to mention the living conditions in Somalia where one in seven children do not finish puberty.

Researchers and governments are working hard, and feverishly, to combat all this, cancer mortality among kids ages under 15 in the U.S. has dropped 71% since the 1970s[118], and in Europe alone 99.55 percent of all children survive their teenage years, but that is cold comfort to those who bury their offspring. Even if you tell them that global average life expectancy rose from under 30 in 1820 to over 70 in 2020, it won't bring their child back. Infant mortality dropped ninety percent during those two centuries. Good luck telling the parents of the other ten percent why that is good news.

Frenchman Pierre Cota was 45 years old when he got involved in a highway backup collision on his way to the Lyon airport on January 20, 1992.[119] His car was totaled, he was taken by ambulance to the hospital where, fortunately, he was quickly released. He missed his plane to Strasbourg, got in a cab to the airport anyway and took the next flight, but that didn't go well either. The Airbus crashed into a Vosges mountainside. Of the 96 people on board, only nine passengers survived the impact. Pierre was one of them. Again he was rushed to a hospital, the second time that day, and again he was found unharmed except for a nosebleed. He made it to his appointment in Strasbourg on time.

Does such an example feed our optimism? The answer is yes. Narrow escapes score high. They fall into the underdog category. People find encouragement and hope in others who manage to avoid something seemingly unavoidable. Being stronger than a force majeure, crawling through the eye of a needle. Japanese generations built an entire culture around finding a way out of an otherwise losing position - karate, sumo and judo are based on taking advantage of another's strength by using it against them.

The reaction of optimism and relief also applies to Tilly's story. When an interview with her and her parents was aired by American broadcaster ABC, titled *Angel of the Beach*, the interviewer said afterwards, "This is a story that gives us all a lot of hope. Because if a ten-year-old girl can save so many people from a tsunami, with just a basic amount of knowledge, then certainly we are all totally capable of that."[120] My suspicion is that in millions of living rooms people were nodding their head.

The facts: the tsunami lasted seven hours, and as many as 230,000 people drowned that Boxing Day in 2004 in coastal areas along the Indian Ocean. Tilly's hundred rescued survivors made up only a tiny fraction of that number. Of Pierre Cota's fellow passengers on Air Inter's Flight 148, ninety percent did not survive the crash. Yet people draw hope from Tilly and Pierre's examples. This is all the more striking against the backdrop of what we reflected on earlier in this book: we all rubberneck at bad news.

***

One of the world's best known and most widely taught examples of the optimism of the underdog is that of 16th-century Holland. Charles V was emperor of the Holy Roman Empire, king of Spain and lord of the Netherlands. The mighty House of Habsburg ruled over a European empire that for the first time in seven hundred years, since Charlemagne, had clawed together its original shape again, draped around France like a chokehold.

Charles was generally popular, born in Ghent, living in Brussels; he spoke Spanish, French, German, Italian, Dutch and Latin. He was Isabella of Castile's grandson. Her daughter Joanna had fallen in love head over heels with a young fellow apparently so attractive in appearance that he was dubbed beautiful Philip, Philip the Handsome. Joanna was very much her mother's daughter. She saw Phil, knew immediately what she wanted, pulled him into a house, slammed the door behind him and declared the two of them married. She was seventeen, he a year older. This was the nest that Charles came from.

Holland was only a limited part of the empire he ruled. But it was the place where money was made. Amsterdam, Antwerp, Bruges, Haarlem, Zwolle, Deventer all benefited from Europe's main rivers flowing into the low country before emptying in the North Sea there. Many of the taxes Charles levied in order to govern were raised by business savvy Holland, or the Seventeen Provinces as they were called at the time. A dynamic country where people learned to read and argue at an early age.

For the art of printing was fast becoming empowering. When in the Holy Roman portion of Charles' empire monk Martin Luther's booklet began its multiple printings march, and discussions erupted, they were not limited to popes and bishops. Everyone wanted to participate, with Holland leading the parade. Dutch print shops sprang up left and right in that sixteenth century, small in scale at first, but steadily larger and more professional as demand for printed matter increased. In the year Charles V celebrated his fortieth birthday, Louis Elzevier was born in Leuven.[121] Almost five centuries later, the printing and publishing house he launched in Leiden is now the largest in the world.[122]

Nowhere did the European protest of those years, the public dissatisfaction with people and ways that were out of date, find a more fertile soil than in the Netherlands. On a fragmented continent in motion, the seventeen provinces became the cradle of civil disobedience. The rest of Europe stood by watching, as if looking for a fatal and self-inflicted accident that was waiting to happen, not yet accustomed to what a broad-based revolt from the bottom up was capable of.

The printing press, the instrument by which freedom of expression was rapidly being compelled, became a crowbar. It disrupted and loosened old structures and manners. Debating across a distance, with ideas and thoughts that were now portable, inspired innovation, and to that Charles V made a contribution of his own. He did what had rarely happened in history until then, he retired. He did not wait until old age made governing impossible. He resigned and made way for a new generation, for the son he had named after his handsome father, Philip II.

However, the son refused to be a product of his modern age. On the contrary, Philip had no patience for pluralism and for the granting of fiscal or religious freedoms. He was a man of the iron fist, of going back to square one, of using brute force as a deterrent. The Dutch became his favorite whipping boy. He ordered the Duke of Alva out of retirement from his palace in Salamanca, built just behind that big square of the Plaza Mayor, and the duke brought his son Frederick with him, a cruel duo. Philip unleashed them both upon Naarden, a city that they burned to the ground, upon Mechelen where all the men were hung upside down naked until they died of hypothermia and where the women were raped, and upon Zutphen where holes were cut in the frozen IJssel river in order to drown hundreds of Zutphen citizens.

The effect was largely counterproductive. The Dutch reacted like David to Goliath. Where others thought: the enemy is so big, he cannot be touched, the Dutch figured: he is so big, we can't miss. Easily said now, almost a platitude, but such was the attitude that resulted from an irrepressible optimism in the Low Countries. It dictated that hope was stronger than the experience gained under the hands of the tyrant. Even the young man who had served as Charles V's personal assistant, the prince of Orange-Nassau, turned to mutiny. William sided with protesting Holland.

The Dutch Water Beggars of the sixteenth century were what most governments today would label terrorists. They did what Alva and Don Frederik did; they murdered and stole. Admiral Piet Hein, who brought Spain to the brink of bankruptcy and caused the price of gold and silver worldwide to rise to absurd levels after capturing Spain's silver fleet, was a privateer. The only reason they are all listed alongside William of Orange in Holland's annals of heroes is that they contributed to their country's war for freedom. They acted out of that indestructible optimism, against oppression.

Seven of the seventeen provinces endured eighty years of warfare and a countless number of their own casualties to finally secure victory. They named themselves the Seven United Netherlands, and their triumph was total. Spain, and by extension Portugal, never again became the world power they had been. The Netherlands ruled the seas for a century, with a fleet of twenty thousand ships that was larger than all other fleets combined. It became the place where more than half of all books, worldwide, were published, an estimated 300 million books in the 17th century[123]. In time, Amsterdam alone counted a hundred publishers and four hundred bookstores[124].

And, perhaps the most far-reaching consequence of the Optimistic Century, Holland single-handedly laid the foundation of what two hundred years later was to become an independent America. Thomas Jefferson wrote the Declaration of Independence, by borrowing from the 16th-century texts of the Union of Utrecht and the Pledge of Abandonment, both Dutch declarations of independence. He penned it on sheets of paper that were imported for the occasion from Dutch papermakers.

***

School teacher Eileen Rence from Wisconsin was delayed for a few hours at Chicago's O'Hare airport, on July 17, 1996, due to bad weather. As a result, she missed her connecting flight to Paris in New York by a few minutes. When she called her daughter to tell her she had not yet left the country, the girl began to cry. She had assumed that mother had actually caught Trans World Airlines Flight 800 on time. That plane crashed into the ocean after takeoff, without Eileen. All 230 people on board died.

Eileen decided to simply take the next TWA flight, a day later, and booked a night at a hotel near New York's JFK airport. There, many victims' relatives and media had also gathered. As soon as the cameras caught sight of the only survivor in the room, all attention immediately went to her. The next morning, Eileen's name appeared in the first paragraph of all newspaper reports.[125]

We celebrate the success of the lone survivor. We keep our fingers crossed for the vault robbers in *Ocean's Eleven* with George Clooney and Brad Pitt. There is something special about a man or woman escaping death or prison. Con man Steven Jay Russell escaped from a Texas prison in 1998 by posing as one of the jailers.[126] When police arrested him anyway, he got himself out on bail by posing as the judge. He was apprehended again, but walked out of jail just the same, this time in the disguise of a doctor. Again he was arrested, and again he made it to freedom, now as a corpse, by faking his death. Jim Carrey made a movie about him in 2009.[127]

It doesn't always end well. Attached to the facade of a building on Berlin's Brunnenstrasse is a sculpture. It depicts an East

German soldier jumping across an accordeon roll of barbed wire, the image taken from a true story. On August 15, 1961, corporal Konrad Schumann jumped from East to West Berlin. The Wall was still under construction, and he had watched that morning as a young woman on the west side handed flowers to her mother across the barrier. It was mother's birthday, and daughter was not allowed to be with her. The corporal realized he was looking at the future, and he didn't like what he saw. He jumped.

It took twenty-eight years for the Wall to come down, and all that time Konrad lived in Bavaria, working at an Audi factory. He had no idea what was going on behind the scenes in his former country, where the waiting time for a Trabant automobile was eight years and where having your own telephone connection could take up to twice that long. He did not know that the state security agency, Stasi, employed more people than the entire East German health care system, neighbors who secretly reported on one another on suspicion of harboring sympathies with a happier world. Konrad had no idea that there were hundreds of thousands of jam jars stored in East Berlin basements containing samples of blouses and underwear, meticulously labeled with names and addresses.[128] The sweat from men's underarms and women's groins was preserved there so that dogs could be unleashed on folks who might one day warrant it.

All this information came to light only after the two Germanies were reunited, and it completely alienated Konrad Schumann from his origins. His former friends and colleagues refused contact with him, nor did he get along with his parents.[129] For years, the corporal had been a symbol of an escape to freedom. The photo of his leap across the barbed wire had gone around the world and had been an inspiration for optimism everywhere. In the country he left behind, this had been held against his friends and family, and caused them trouble.

Konrad Schumann became depressed and hung himself from a tree in his Bavarian backyard on June 20, 1998. He had never really found freedom.

Chapter 16

How to achieve a goal, by Texas's Sandra Brown and Maine's Frances Perkins

Optimism instilled by large groups

It is not only loners who, as underdogs, feed a crowd's optimism. Crowds themselves have done it too, throughout the centuries. William of Nassau inherited the French principality of Orange from a cousin who died young and childless on a battlefield. The name had nothing to do with the color, nor with the citrus fruits that grew there, but with an ancient Gallic deity, Arausio. That didn't stop the prince's followers, then and in all the centuries since, from making orange the color of an underdog. Sporting events worldwide leave no doubt as to where in the stands the Dutch fans are. They support the underdog. Pending winning gold, every team and athlete is an underdog.

There's no doubt a crowd can bring optimism to individuals. Earlier we noted the daily well-wishers' demonstration outside Hasbro Children's Hospital in Providence, Rhode Island.[130] That began as a one-man action by a health care provider who once said goodbye to a young patient who was to be discharged the next day. Therapist Steven Brosnihan is a cyclist, and the bike route home ran past the child's window. He stopped, flashed his lamp, and the patient briefly flashed the room light in return.

Steven decided to do something similar for more patients, and as other road users heard about it, they joined in, every night at 8:30. Just wishing goodnight. When Covid broke out, the greeting extended to also include nursing staff, and now police patrol cars, ships passing by on the Providence River, walkers with cell phones, and store front lights nearby also join in. The children in the hospital love it; it encourages them.[131]

Or this example, from Turkey. Muharrem Yazgan is deaf, he lives in Istanbul. On December 24, 2014, he took his sister Ozlem shopping, because when you're hearing impaired in Turkey, navigating the crowded streets and stores by yourself can be challenging. Hardly anyone masters Turkish sign language, but Ozlem does. They walked into a bagel store, and suddenly the man behind the counter gestured with his hands that he had hot bagels today. Muharrem was pleasantly surprised. Outside, someone dropped a bag with groceries, Muharrem helped pick them up, and the man thanked him in sign language. A woman bumped into him and gestured that she was apologizing.

A Youtube video that has now been viewed millions of times shows what was happening. Phone company Samsung had set up a video call-in center specifically for deaf people and wanted to raise awareness of it. With the help of his sister, they found a teacher who, unbeknownst to Muharrem, spent weeks teaching the neighborhood sign language. On that one day, everyone brother and sister encountered on the street addressed Muharrem in his own language.[132] Look it up, watch for yourself, and see how he reacts when he discovers how the entire neighborhood is trying, literally, to lend him a hand.

***

And then there's the crowds that encourage optimism of the crowds themselves. The example that had the most far reaching implications comes from 18th-century America, which, following the Dutch example, declared its own independence. It also borrowed the name: the Republic of the United Provinces became the Republic of the United States. And it inspired others. Frenchmen who fought along with the American insurgents told people back home that liberation was possible, even in France. A comparison between the English king and his French counterpart was quickly made, and France disposed of Louis XVI. This led to explosions of violence, and to an outright dictatorship under Napoleon, but in the long run the ideals of liberty, equality and fraternity survived, not only in France, but elsewhere in Europe as well.

That said, in the U.S. it took a while for organizing its independence before it got on a solid track. Contrary to what most history books suggest, it did not immediately lead to a constitution that gave citizens the rights for which the Americans are now known worldwide. Twelve years passed between independence and the adoption of the constitution. When the thirteen founding states finally got to see the draft of the text, they were shocked. The only thing it really settled were the rights and duties of government. It answered political questions that had long been debated, but the rights of the citizenry were nowhere to be seen.

About representation of the people: is each state allotted the same number of delegates or is the number in proportion to how many people live in a state? The compromise was: same number in the Senate, proportional in the House. Taxes: states with more people pay more taxes than more sparsely populated states, but are slaves included in the count? Compromise: for that purpose, a slave counts as a three-fifths person. Slave trade: abolish the importing of new slaves or not? Compromise: yes, but not until twenty years from now. Presidents: for how long can someone be head of state? Unanimous: for periods of four years at a time.

But ask anyone today anywhere, in America or abroad, what the most notable parts of the U.S. Constitution are, and they'll say: freedom of speech, freedom of the press, freedom of religion, separation of church and state, the right to bear firearms, equal rights for all. And it's true, those are all part of the Constitution. But none of that was in the original text submitted to the states for approval in 1788.

Men of the caliber of George Washington, James Madison, Benjamin Franklin and John Jay, for whom the town of Jay, Maine is named, great figures in history, had come up with the text. Their job was to assure that America's fundamentals were not to be anything like how the English government was set up, the country from which the states had seceded, and the draft did indeed take care of that. America became a republic, with clearly defined checks and balances. But it did not include the rights of individual citizens.

Protests were rampant. On the one hand, there were the governors of the thirteen states themselves who wanted to keep the federal government at as far a distance as possible. They were supported by their own fellow state citizens. They too didn't want a national government that could infringe on their personal freedoms. They figured: if we are going to have our own country now, where we can start with a clean slate, let's do it properly and thoroughly. And before the creators of the new constitution realized it, their creation was in danger of being rejected everywhere - for most people it didn't go far enough.

The euphoria that had followed the declaration of independence in 1776 and the expulsion of the British army in the years thereafter had not made the young America a perfect nation. But it did make it a nation of citizens who increasingly spoke up. There were large groups that had no appetite at all for a strong central government. To them, that seemed too much like the kind of power the English king had, which was precisely what they had liberated themselves from. They also feared that a federal government would too often sit in the judge's chair. In a young country where distances were still lengthy and calculated in numbers of a day's travel on horseback, there was no desire for a long arm from afar.

All this turmoil worried the writers of the constitutional text, for two reasons. The first was that everyone had yet to get used to what exactly it was: a democracy. Alexander Hamilton expressed concern about "an excess of democracy,"[133] others spoke of "democratical tyranny"[134] and "republican frenzy."[135] Essays were published, for and against the constitution, printed in newspapers, later called the Federal Papers, and at times the debates were rowdy. That was the second cause for concern. What if there were so many divisions that there would be no constitution at all? Then the cornerstone under the new country would fall away, with all the risks that would cause. There was a provisional constitution, since independence was declared, but it dealt mainly with the internal rights of each state. With that, America could not move forward in the long run.

And so the advocates of retaining as much state power as possible as well as the advocates of acquiring as many individual citizen rights as possible found each other in a joint protest against the proposed constitution. Both groups encouraged each other and gave each other hope. The result was that the drafters returned to the drawing table with a promise of making adjustments and additions, and the promise was kept. It was a compromise that everyone could finally live with. The original text was approved by all thirteen states on the condition that they could within two years vote on twelve additions. The constitution would then be rewritten, with the changes incorporated, but instead the decision was made that the core text would stay as is, and that the additions would be attached, as an appendix, as amendments.

These were collectively called the Bill of Rights, supplementary legislation that gave the conservative states the assurance that they retained full control over anything not expressly included in the powers of the central government. And proponents of individual rights obtained their freedom of religion, speech, printing press, assembly, home security, the right to own firearms, as well as a handful of detailed rights to impartial justice without excessive penalties or bail amounts. Ten of the twelve amendments passed. An amendment that restricted pay raises for House members did not gain sufficient support among the states until two hundred years later. And an attempt to incorporate the number of Congress members in the Constitution failed for good.

The U.S. Constitution, thus amended in 1791, has since been one of the clearest examples of effective group optimism, a take-action optimism that results in its intended consequences. Despite the diversity among those that found the original legal text deficient, each with their own motives and preferences, they encouraged each other. It propelled the speed of action and decisions.

The only group that remained gagged for the time being were Black people. They were not given a voice until seventy years later, after a civil war and the abolition of slavery, with imperfections in the South at first, but securing that no one was any longer only sixty percent human. Not gagged, but without access to the ballot box, was a much larger group, American women. They had to wait until 1920.

* * *

Sandra Brown is one of the most successful writers of all time. Nearly one hundred million books in print, translated into 34 languages, number one on the New York Times best-sellers list more than fifty times. She and I are ten months apart, we both started in local journalism, she as a weather woman at a TV station in Texas, I at a newspaper in Europe. I talked to her in the summer of 2017 about the type of woman she usually writes about.

She is a woman like all women, she said, comparing her to the classic female described in myths and stories throughout the ages. "The typical myth, about a very reluctant protagonist, someone who, whatever challenge greets them, they immediately refuse it, they want no part of it, like: leave me alone, I'm fine where I am, that kind of attitude. But then they seize upon the opportunity or the challenge and over the course of the story, they give it their all to try and achieve their goal after all."

In that nutshell, Sandra painted women everywhere who initially reluctantly took up the fight to demand their equal rights. They had always been listened to, century after century. In Roman and Greek antiquity, they appeared in mythologies as strong, powerful goddesses. And as we saw, in the Middle Ages, step by step, and on the chessboard move by move, they began to co-rule. But the last word almost always stayed with men.

During the Civil War, three million men were called to the fronts. Their day jobs were mostly taken over by women. When the men returned, they wanted their jobs back. This didn't go over well with the women. They resisted being pushed back into the kitchen. At the same time, during that second half of the nineteenth century, the quality of their education rose sharply. Many girls finished school, and more and more of them sought further education. It resulted in one generation of empowered women after another.

The economy discovered that women became a serious market segment. Their clothes changed. Frances Folsom, the young bride of President Grover Cleveland, 21 years old, in 1886 tore the bustle from her dresses, and many women followed her example[136]. Women-only magazines came out, and the American woman began appearing on front pages, in color. She was called the New Woman and was soon labeled a feminist, or she was a Gibson Girl, the modern type of a self-confident young woman that illustrator Charles Gibson put on page one each month of a magazine that expressed the times, The Ladies Home Journal.

Increasingly, she was found with a drink in her hand on an outdoor café terrace, debating, or in a park, arguing. She spoke with contempt, and over time with anger, about men who at the end of the week squandered their wages at the bar, before coming home drunk and flat broke. And so she started two protest movements, one to get alcohol banned, the other for her own right to vote. She won on both fronts, overwhelmingly, and with a conviction that was the effect of her optimism. By the time a new century dawned, there was no doubt, women were getting the same rights as men.

Author Sandra Brown described the process women went through and summed it up for me in one sentence, because that way, she said, she herself had learned the difficult, demanding craft of being a successful storyteller. "Your heart can be all in it, but you still have to study, you still have to work really hard, to finally get it done." And then it doesn't need to be all perfect at first, because you'll go back to it and do your editing, your rewriting, "I am a big rewriter." Maine's Stephen King echoes that approach, stressing the necessity of doing the hard work. "Sometimes you have to go on when you don't feel like it, and sometimes you're doing good work when it feels like all you're managing is to shovel shit from a sitting position." It made him view the Carrie character in his book totally differently over time as he kept working at it, for one's "original perception of a character or characters may be as erroneous as" anyone else's until you have given it your all.[137]

Women had their way, and serving alcohol became constitutionally banned. It didn't work, though. Most people, men and women alike, managed to hold on to their bottles regardless, and wouldn't let go of their moments of tipping their glass. Back to the drawing board, back to the rewrite. Fourteen years later, prohibition was removed from the Constitution after all.

***

Which happened to coincide with the arrival of Fannie Perkins in Washington, as the nation's first female cabinet secretary. Born of two Maine parents, she pronounced her job as Secretary of *Lay-bah*. She was forty years old by the time she could finally vote, and wasted no energy in bemoaning her gender. "Being a woman has only bothered me in climbing trees," she stated. She shed Fannie, replaced it with Frances, and off she went making a difference. Frances Perkins became the longest serving labor secretary in U.S. history and a key architect of Franklin Roosevelt's New Deal policies. She helped implement the 40-hour work week, minimum wage, overtime pay, unemployment insurance, work safety standards, social security, workman's comp, as well as the right to the weekend off.[138]

After she was done, twelve years later, she retired to the Perkins homestead in Newcastle that had been a family property for more than two centuries, forever an optimist about what one individual can achieve for many. "I came to Washington," she said, "to work for God, FDR, and the millions of forgotten, plain common workingmen." When asked by the end of her life what, of all this work, her proudest achievement was, her reply consisted of four words, "Two words: Social Security."[139]

Chapter 17

Going bananas, ice, and free books in Maine

Optimism and pioneering

No one ever goes to sea on a lobster boat expecting to be miserable. No lobsterman, male or female, believes that the ocean won't provide. Yes, there are government regulations that they dislike and mandatory paperwork that they hate, and they suspect that the bureaucrats who make the rules know nothing, zilch, about fishing for a living. Worst case, this makes them annoyed, irritated, angry at times. But no, none of the roughly five thousand Maine lobstermen is a pessimist. In fact, each of them is an optimist. They realistically expect to land their lobsters, as they always have.

Say "Maine", and people everywhere unfailingly react with "lobster". After having traveled every U.S. state with the exception of Maine, Alice and I, while having dinner in a Maryland Red Lobster restaurant, decided to finally go see it. We went, and we stayed. Not for the lobster, though. For our first Maine dinner we actually did have lobster chowder, in Lubec, but the thing that truly grabbed our attention was a library. The little one in Fort Kent, at the far end of U.S. Route 1.

I knew Todd Bol, I had interviewed him a few months earlier at a librarians convention in Chicago, and we had stayed in touch since. Not many folks recognize his name today, but he was the guy behind that tiny library on Fort Kent's Hall Street. Todd from Hudson, Wisconsin loved his mom, an educator who had dedicated her adult life to teaching children to read. After she passed, in 2009 Todd dismantled an old garage door and built what to most people looked like a dollhouse, but was in fact a mini schoolhouse, a class room. He placed it on a stick in his front yard and filled it with used books. Anyone walking by could open the little door and take one home, at no charge. Borrowers were expected to return the book later, or keep it and replace it with another book. Todd Bol had started the Little Free Libraries.

He often quoted Martin Luther who was once asked what he'd do if he knew that tomorrow would be his final day on Earth. Answer, "Plant a seed." Todd did. He died in 2018, too young, but he lived long enough to see that his nonprofit made it to Reader's Digest's *"50 Surprising Reasons We Love America."*[140] Bruce Springsteen and Jon Bon Jovi ranked number 50, Bill Gates was at 25, and on spot 11, right behind sliced bread, were the little free libraries. Fort Kent has one, the Presque Isle/Caribou area counts ten, there are forty little free libraries in and around Bangor, forty-two in Augusta, and fifty in Portland. In all, hundreds and hundreds of Mainers have put tiny book-filled schoolhouses on sticks in their front yards.

Each one is an expression of optimism that doing something nice, something good, without expecting anything in return, will generate a positive outcome. Such as neighbors meeting neighbors, folks who live around the corner suddenly stopping and greeting each other while browsing what's in that library, sometimes after years of never really having known one another. Or book lovers finally finding that old title that they were never able to dig up in the used book store.

***

Maine was love at first sight. But then, how do you cross the Piscataqua River bridge into Kittery and not immediately sense something different? Three hundred miles until the end of I-95, and all you are going to see is trees. And water. Before long, we drove parallel to, then crossed, the Kennebec, outside Maine a mostly forgotten river, but still revered at home. Many Americans know about Bath, at the river mouth. There was a time when every two weeks or so Bath Iron Works would launch a new destroyer for the U.S. Navy, and today the storied shipyard still ranks high in the world's top ten. But when we spotted the Kennebec, we didn't think ships. We went bananas.

I mentioned earlier that I consider my adopted home state one of the most optimistic places in the world, and here is one reason why. In the old days, no one outside the southern states ever saw a banana, let alone they knew what it tasted like. Until the Kennebec came to the rescue. A little over a hundred years ago, Maine had become the nation's number one provider of frozen water, and almost all of that ice came from the Kennebec. Each winter, the river would freeze over with 18 or more inches of crystal clear, solid ice, which was then expertly cut, collected, stored in icehouses in stacks that reached to the rafters, and handled by farm boys or lumberjacks or deckhands with special winter job titles. They were chiselers, barmen, breakers, or shovelers who were better known as *chip Joes* or, my favorite, *banjo artists*. They all kept the ice blocks clean and separated, and insulated against melting with generous helpings of Maine sawdust.

Maine's ice kept New York cool during summers, as well as Boston, Philadelphia, Washington and most other big cities along the East coast. City bars served "smashes", cocktails on smashed Maine ice, while inside the White House food was kept constantly refrigerated in a building where summers could be unbearable. After president James Garfield was shot on July 2, 1881 at a train depot where he collapsed in the arms of Secretary of State James Blaine from Augusta, temperatures in his White House bedroom exceeded 90 degrees. Engineers placed crates with Maine ice in an adjacent room, and installed a fan that blew air over the ice, into a tube that led into Garfields room. It made his final days considerably more comfortable before the president eventually died from his wounds. It was the first known attempt at creating an air conditioning system.[141]

Maine ice was transported in schooners, and to inland destinations by train, hundreds, sometimes thousands, of miles away. That's how it ended up in ports such as New Orleans where bananas had just arrived from Central America, ready to introduce the rest of the United States to a fruit they had heard about but never seen. It was a major success. As it turned out, for conserving their foods, fruits and drinks during spring and summer communities east of the Mississippi would rely on Kennebec ice during all the years between the start of the Civil War and the end of World War I.

Who were these guys? Regular Mainers whose farm jobs were paused during the winter months, whose lobster boats didn't go out to sea, and whose forests were covered with too much snow to allow for fulltime lumber work. They were not going to sit down twiddling their thumbs. Eventually, at a four-mile stretch alone of the frozen Kennebec there would be 4,000 men and 350 horses working day and night. There were thirty-six ice companies along the bottom end of the river, with fifty-three ice-houses that could hold more than a million tons of ice. The U.S. Census Bureau decided to look into it. They were astounded to see that "from Bath to Hallowell there is now more capital concentrated [...] than in any other locality of equal extent in the world," a distance of a mere thirty miles.[142]

Having acces to an abundance of land, trees, and water, Mainers have always known exactly what to do to make it work for them and others. What has helped was that migration into Maine all but stopped by the end of the Civil War, when farmers moved to greener pastures in the Midwest. Moreover, land ownership in Maine has historically been much more private than federal, which has led to a healthy local stewardship of land and forests. Remarkably, there is just about the same Maine acreage covered by forest today as there was a thousand years ago.[143]

All this is the result of people keeping an eye on tomorrow, of always making an effort to calibrate the effect that what they do today will have on tomorrow and the day after, and on the generation thereafter. All that, and never ceasing to innovate and re-innovate. Hence Maine's use of the Kennebec ice, and their insistence to be paid both with dollars and with coal to keep themselves warm in the winter. When schooner captains were asked what business they were in, they'd say that they were "ice and coaling."

Smart.

The larger story is this: Maine had showed the world that modern nations could not do without refrigeration. Abraham Lincoln's Union troops, often fighting and moving far from big cities, kept being reliably fed with food that was supplied to them by rail, in refrigerated wagons kept cool with ice from Maine. And as America's population grew explosively once the war was over, food could no longer be wasted by allowing it to spoil - it needed preservation by refrigeration. Therefore, in line with humanity's history of always seeking ways and means of improving the status quo, it was only a matter of time before household refrigerators arrived on America's Main Street.

Maine's ice success story ended with a bang. On June 29, 1910 an icehouse on the bank of the Kennebec caught fire, likely caused by a spark from a passing train. Icehouses catching fire was always a risk waiting to materialize because the wooden buildings were kept bone dry year-round. A strong wind fanned the flames to two schooners that were loading ice which was to travel south in order to chill summer life in sweating cities. One schooner, as good as fully loaded, sat aground waiting for high tide to lift her up, and was therefore immovable. The other hurried away from the wharf but got her anchor stuck. Both vessels burned to the water. Several icehouses burned as well, and 40,000 tons of ice were lost. The US Army Corps of Engineers came out to open up the river for traffic.[144] They got it done by late October, just in time before the Kennebec would freeze, but the damage done to the industry was considerable.

It heralded the end of Maine's admirable and pioneering ice trade, by way of what historian Gavin Weightman described as "a spectacular Viking funeral."[145]

By 1950, thanks to Maine and far ahead of the rest of the world, 90 percent of Americans living in towns as well as 80 percent of their rural neighbors made their own ice in refrigerators at home.

Chapter 18

"Do not worry about tomorrow"

Faith based optimism

Who am I more like today, do I feel like Thomas? Like Jean-Jacques? Or Pollyanna? Probably not Pollyanna. She would handle this moment better. Definitely not like Thomas Hobbes. His pessimism is four centuries old, and so often quoted that it has fallen flat.[146] Moreover, life is not "solitary, poor, nasty, brutish, and short," as he wrote, at least not the lives of the vast majority of people on Earth. Jean-Jacques Rousseau, also cited with excessive frequency, perhaps comes closer to this moment: reality has its limits, but the world of imagination is boundless, he said.[147] This, after all, is why I find myself with my crew in Puerto Montt. If it wasn't for boundless imagination, we would not have started this whole thing, we would never have taken off in the helicopter.

There were many who had advised against it. A Robinson-44 weighs thirteen hundred pounds, empty. That's about as light as my first car in 1971, a red Citroen 2CV made in France, locally known as an Ugly Duckling. "Would you do it?" I over-

156

heard one pilot asking another, a few days before we took off. "Absolutely not." Like we were out of our minds. Flying forty thousand miles in a sardine can, across water, mountains, a desert, jungles, over guerrilla barracks, and across twenty-nine national borders, in all types of weather. It had never been done before, no, and as far as the skeptics were concerned that had a very good reason. Too risky, too dangerous.

They were quite right not to dare it. Those who shy away from an undertaking fraught with so many uncertain factors, with predictable but mainly unpredictable confrontations with the goddess of adventure and the devil of challenge, ought to never try a thing like this. They don't provoke the stars, they fear the risks, and they would therefore be more prone to making mistakes. Smart pilots, and almost all of them are, pride themselves on the principle that prudence is the mother of their cockpit. When in doubt, stay on the ground.

As for myself, I assessed the risk of the venture differently, as manageable. Mainly because flying long distances, including super-long distances, consists of flying short distances. A helicopter is not in the air for three hundred hours at a stretch, but for three hours, at most. On the ground in Los Angeles, I didn't worry about landing in Buenos Aires. Our only concern there was to get safely to San Diego, the next stop an hour and a half away. Ditto at the Acapulco airport a few days later, I had no worries about the weather forecast in Panama. That landing was still eight days away. In Acapulco, our only concern was covering the distance of 250 miles to Huatulco, a two-and-a-half hour flight under sunny skies. Not only is this the only workable approach, it is also the only real one.

Matthew of Galilee is said to have put into words, two thousand years ago, one of optimism's main components. "Do not worry about tomorrow."[148] That is not to say that tomorrow couldn't be a cause for concern, for "each day has enough trouble of its own," but "tomorrow will worry about itself." He put it into practice. Matthew was a tax collector; he had a fine income, he made good money. But he gave up the job, in exchange for an uncertain existence as a stagehand in the road show of a rock star who claimed he could turn water into wine and pluck bread from the sky. No idea what tomorrow may or may not bring, but Matthew wasn't going to worry about it.

It was and is guidance that has stood the test of time pretty well. People wake up to a new sunrise every morning. No one, or at least hardly anyone, stays in bed depressed with a feeling that the whole getting up thing is pointless because, after all, within a matter of hours the sun will set again anyway. That's of later concern, we know. There is a new day, a new opportunity, so get up, roll up your sleeves. One day at a time. Or in our case: one flight at a time.

Rousseau had it right, reality comes with limitations. In Puerto Montt, in southern Chile, twelve hundred miles south from where earlier we had been stuck with an engine mishap at a gas station on a roadside, we had to choose. From the moment we had entered South America, by crossing from Panama into Colombia, we had the ocean on our right, and the Andes mountains on our left. It is a very long ridge, at almost six thousand miles the longest in the world. Tall peaks, averaging twelve thousand feet above sea level, too high for the helicopter to fly across. High air is thin, and thin air makes for less lift. What we were looking for was a stretch of mountains not twelve thousand feet high, but four thousand feet, three times lower. That you find at Puerto Montt.

The distance to Bariloche, on the other side of the Andes, and also on the other side of the Chilean-Argentinean border, is a hundred and twenty miles. It is not in any way a straight line. It is a path between two steep, frozen and snow-covered cliff walls, with many angles, twists and turns, sometimes flying low over bluffs, sometimes high above a precipice. It is maneuvering through a stretched-out, nonstop winding mountain pass where you can never be sure from which direction the wind is going to come next. Wind in the mountains comes not only from the left, right, front or back, but also from above as airflows are pushed down over a ridge. Mountain flying requires experience. Mountain flying in the equivalent of a French Ugly Duckling requires supreme concentration. All the factors, all the conditions, all the details, that all has to come together. And that's on a good day.

In Puerto Montt, we did not have a good day. Sunny weather along the coast, but as soon as the Osorno volcano came in sight and we turned left, into the Andes, low-hanging clouds could already be seen everywhere. At the point where the mountain pass begins, near the small town of Peulla, a thick curtain of fog served as a bouncer: entry denied. The helicopter flew us back to the airport where it had taken off earlier, and I checked ourselves in again because anyone planning to fly across the border has to check themselves out first, by getting the mandatory go-aheads from emigration and customs officials. The night was spent in town, in what a sign at the reception said was "the southernmost Holiday Inn in the world."

As far as "all has to come together," the next day was not a good one either. This time there was a strong wind, with snow and hail. Helicopters don't care for hail. The ice pellets hit the rotor blades with the speed at which they spin, nearly five hundred miles per hour. The skin of rotor blades is thin, made of a relatively fragile steel laminate. It's like shooting at it with a BB gun. Therefore, as soon as a hailstorm comes into view, a helicopter gets out of the way. We parked on a lake shore, sitting on black sand compliments of the volcano, and waited for half an hour, with the engine running. Any longer was unwise, or there would be insufficient fuel in the tanks for making it all the way through and across the mountains. The weather didn't let up, so again back to town we went, back to the officials. I decided to not check ourselves in again this time.

The morning of day three, upon arrival at the airport the crew was immediately stopped by the passport stamp guy who said that what I did yesterday was not acceptable. He looked serious and he was right. I expressed regret and had us stamped twice, in and out again. Started to say that every day at our hotel we also had to check in and out, each time assuming we wouldn't return that night, but I bit my tongue. The man did his job, and from the looks of it, he did it thoroughly. None of it helped us anyway. The Andes were once again completely locked. A new approach route, over yesterday's lake, did us no good for inevitably the helicopter had to pass by that village, Peulla, the front gate of the mountain pass. And this fog curtain was still hanging there, thick and fat. Three times was not a charm.

This was the reason why I was asking myself the questions. Who did I feel like? Hobbes? Rousseau? Or Pollyanna? The Andes sometimes look like a really vicious mountain range. They are ancient mountains, the Earth's oldest except for the Urals, and it shows. Peaks that often seem like sharp serrated knives, abrased by wind and weather. Ragged edges, nowhere a plateau where you can safely set down a helicopter in case of an emergency. Beautiful, very pretty, picture perfect through Sigurveig's camera lens, but grim. Attempted to cross it three times, failed three times. I had visions of the filmed flight of a Uruguayan plane that crashed into an Andes mountainside in 1972, on a Friday the 13th. With survivors who stayed alive by eating the flesh of dead co-passengers.[149]

Perhaps this was the end point. Ushuaia, the intended destination at the very southernmost tip of the continent, the capital of what Argentina calls her province of Antarctica, was still another twelve hundred miles to go. Sometimes you don't get what you want, sometimes you can't scrape the bottom.

Don't force it, is the motto, don't defy fate. "Maybe this is not meant to be?" No, yelled Thomas Hobbes. He never had much use for Matthew. Hobbes preferred leaning on the preacher who four centuries before Galilee's tax collector claimed that everything is vanity, "chasing after the wind" and, moreover, "wearisome." What do people gain, spoke the cynic, "from all their labors at which they toil under the sun?"[150] Turn around, and go home.

Pollyanna, however, was of a very different opinion. She is the orphan girl in Eleanor Porter's children's book, a darling child who sees the sunny side of everything.[151] Pollyanna has been the eternal optimist since in 1913 she was breathed life into, so much so that she was quickly proclaimed an archetype. In that capacity she is usually described as incorrigible, as someone seeing pluses where only minuses can reasonably be expected. In Miss Porter's book however, she is more realistic. There, she is blessed with a tendency that all humans have shown throughout the ages.

In psychology, the Pollyanna Principle stands for an urge to hide unpleasant memories behind better ones. The "good old days" are an expression of the Pollyanna Principle, the memory of a past in which much, if not everything, was better. The memory is incorrect. Every old time was objectively worse than now, unhealthier, unsafer, unfriendlier, more threatening, people got sick faster, died younger, earned less, and inequality was greater. The tendency to remember the opposite is usually an expression of pessimism, not optimism. In it, the old times contrast positively with the present, let alone the future.

The attitude of the original Pollyanna, in the book and later in the movie with Hayley Mills and Jane Wyman, is a different one. She expects that things are going to work out, even against indications to the contrary, but she accepts that outcomes can yet disappoint. The story was a huge success, with large print runs and sequel books, and with an Oscar for

Hayley Mills. People easily, and willingly, identify with some-one like Pollyanna. They want her high hopes for the future. That's optimism.

In Puerto Montt, however, I didn't dare to trust the girl just like that. The weather was bad, it was the dead of winter, the terrain was completely unknown, even threatening here and there, and in case of an emergency we would be unreachable for a rescue in the middle of the mountains anyway, even though we were carrying a satellite phone. What Thomas Hobbes was whispering to me did not sound unreasonable under the circumstances. Was I playing with three lives? Was setting a record worth this kind of risk? Besides, what is a world record anyway - and again Hobbes quoted the old preacher, "There is nothing new under the sun." Also, I didn't feel I was cut out to be a potential cannibal.

So where was Jean-Jacques Rousseau when you needed him? He was a romantic, he had a sense for this kind of expedition. He was Swiss, that also helped; they are not easily extreme. We talked earlier about the U.S. Constitution, well, Rousseau in-spired a good part of the French one, about rights and liberties of man. Without him there would have been no Universal Dec-laration of Human Rights two hundred years later, at least not so clearly articulated. Rousseau believed that human motives are fundamentally sound, and that we come into the world as well-intentioned beings, but we have the tendency and an urge to screw up.

Jean-Jacques was over a century younger than Thomas, and quite a bit older than Pollyanna. So he was somewhere in the middle, but this was at the same time also the problem. With Rousseau, I could go either way. He had urinary problems all his life, issues with his bladder or his prostate, maybe the kidneys. He was often ill because of it, and in a lot of pain. No idea if and how that affected his judgment, let alone whether it could help advise me on my anxious question: do I dare to cross the Andes?

I decided to share my anxiety with the one I trusted most, and so I called Alice. I told her about our failed attempts, about the wind, the snow, the hail, about the dark, dense clouds, the water and the steep mountain walls. About how we felt like we were flying blind, unable to see any openings in the cloud cover, any cracks between mountain and cloud, a patch of blue through which we might see the sun. About that little town of Peulla where the passage had been jammed shut for three days. "I'm scared," I confessed.

That was for the first time. Nothing else had been really frightening along the way so far. It hadn't exactly been all smooth sailing, for in the air as well as on the ground things do get turbulent in a variety of ways often enough, but never of such a nature that we had no idea how it was eventually going to be resolved. Optimism had not let me down anywhere at any time. But now I wasn't so sure about it all; this was perfectly uncharted territory, figuratively and especially literally, and I had only one word for what I was feeling. Fear. Part of me hoped Alice would say: turn around, come home.

What she did say, was: now go get a good night's sleep first. Tomorrow everything may be different. That's what mornings sometimes do. And then you make a decision, not before. Because now in the dark you can't decide anything, nor do you need to.

***

On the fourth day, the next morning, the sun was shining, radiantly. We checked out, filled the tanks, and took off. Past the Osorno that smiled at us. Under a cloudless sky, up to Peulla that we now saw clearly below us for the first time. The passage into the mountains lay wide open. Between the peaks, clouds were lingering, many of them, some thick and gray, but always we could see a crack of blue sky somewhere. As long as we kept that in sight, the sun was shining.

All it took was two hours, and the helicopter was on the ground in Bariloche, on the other side of the Andes. An Argentine immigration officer broke into a smile as he stamped my Dutch passport. "Maxima," he said, referring to Holland's Argentina-born queen.

Twelve hundred miles and six days later, in Ushuaia looking at a wooden sign that said *Fin del mundo*, the end of the world, I was talking to Alice again. I asked what she remembered from our phone conversation that night in Puerto Montt. She said, "'Turn around!' is what I wanted to shout at you, 'come home!' I was even more scared than you were. But I wouldn't have helped you with that." She was absolutely right, and I told her so, at the edge of the end of the world. It was July 13 that day, a Friday.

Chapter 19

The golden day of tomorrow

The optimism of pursuing something shiny

People pursue. Whether it is a personal record, or knowledge, a career, the heart of someone they have fallen in love with, or wealth, they unfailingly tell themselves they are pursuing happiness. It is always an expression of optimism, and always has been, throughout ten thousand years of large-brained history. But it is even more than that, science tells us, in particular when we are pursuing shiny objects.

We appreciate the look of glossy magazines better than matte ones. Advertising on glossy paper is more appealing than marketing something on paper that doesn't shine. Even young children who do not distinguish between expensive and inexpensive products, prefer the one that is shown on glossy paper. Why is that? Why are we attracted to chrome? And why to gold?

Let me take you to the world of gold for a moment, as it offers an easily recognizable example of this type of fascination.

No one turns pessimistic from window shopping at a jeweler's store. Gold has an attraction that we cannot easily put into words, but that yet has the same effect as waking up, looking out the window to say hello to a sunrise, and smelling the aroma of the day's first cup of coffee.

In chemistry, *Au* is the symbol for gold, *aurum* in Latin. It is derived from a word the ancient Romans used for daybreak, aurora, a new dawn, the day of tomorrow. The word gold itself comes from the Middle Dutch word *gelo*, which became yellow in English, and *geel* in Dutch. Gold is the only yellow-colored metal produced by the Earth, hence its relationship with the rising sun, the new day. It is also one of the rarest metals. The low supply explains in part the high level of demand.

All the gold mined since its discovery still exists today. It does not dissolve, it can be mixed with other metals temporarily but not permanently, because it never disappears or spoils, and it is exceptionally ductile. You can stretch a nugget of thirty grams of gold into a wire fifty miles long, but you can also flatten it into a 100-square-ft sheet if you wish.[152] This is why a wedding ring made of 24-karat gold is a bad idea - too soft to last a marriage intact. To prevent bumps, dents and deformation, more solid materials are attached to it, hence the lower carats.

If we could weigh all the gold in the world together, the meter on the scale would tip to 275 million pounds. How much is that? The U.S. steel industry produces 275 million pounds of steel within a three-hour time frame. Mined gold took six thousand years to reach that weight. Additionally, it is twice as heavy as steel: in terms of volume, all the gold in the world would easily fit inside the hold of one oil tanker.

Gold makes hopeful; everyone wants it, as a ring, a bracelet or as an investment, as a bar safely tucked away in a safe deposit box. Kings and queens make it into a crown and put it on their heads, despite its weight. Egyptians were the first to get their hands on it, around four millennia BC, letting Nubians do the digging, and the only reason they gave them that name was because *nub* was the Egyptian word for gold. By the time Moses received the ten commandments on the mountain, gold was abundant: God prescribed to him in minute detail how the tabernacle and its furnishings were to be beautified with gold, turning that part of the Bible into a meticulous 121-verse manual.[153]

Gold is permanent; it has an eternal life. That's a second reason for its never-ending demand. Gold reminds people of what they would like to be but are not, immortal, unbeatable, indestructible. Even after all the steel in the world has crumbled and rusted away, your gold pendant will still exist, shiny as new. Generations across thousands of years have told each other stories about the hunt for gold, even though the hunting has frequently led to disappointment. English author John Ruskin wrote two centuries ago about a man who had converted his entire property into gold coins. He went on a journey with it, boarded a ship, which then wrecked in a storm. The man grabbed his bag of gold, jumped overboard and sank like a stone. "Did he have the gold?" asked Ruskin, "or did the gold have him?"[154]

Good question, who has the gold? In a Manhattan building sandwiched between Nassau Street and William Street, there is a vault five stories below ground level. In it are an estimated half a million gold bars. They belong to the International Monetary Fund (IMF) and the central banks of more than 30 countries, excluding the U.S. itself but including most major Western European economies. Those countries pay each other or the IMF for goods and services with gold. After each transaction, a man or woman walks into the vault, and they move bars covering the transaction amount to another spot inside the same vault. The gold never leaves the vault itself, let alone the building. It merely changes virtual ownership, a few or many bars at a time, but the owner himself never sees the gold. Who has it?

***

Outside the harbor of the Greek city of Volos, a monument refers to an ancient story that circulated three thousand years ago, before Homer's time. The king of Boeotia had divorced his first wife and then remarried. His son Phryxus was being bullied by his stepmother. The real mother felt sorry for him and she arranged for Phryxus and his sister Helle an early version of a helicopter, a ram with wings. Its hairy skin was covered in gold. The ram took off for a flight across water and mountains, from the Greek mainland all the way to the other side of the Black Sea.

Helle became airsick and fell into the water between two shores, a spot today appearing on maps and charts as the Hellespont. Her brother made it through. After landing, he sacrificed the ram to Zeus and gave the remains to the local king who then nailed the gold-covered hide to a tree, and hired a fire-breathing dragon to guard it. It became known far and wide as the Golden Fleece.

Volos is situated at the foothills of the Pelion Mountains. They were named for King Pelias who was concerned about the popularity of his nephew Jason who was after his throne. Pelias promised Jason his golden scepter, but in return he had to first bring him the Golden Fleece - an impossible task, he figured. Jason set sail in Volos with a ship full of rowers, the Argonauts, and survived the crossing to the far end of the Black Sea. There he seduced the daughter of the king who had put up the fleece, Medea, and she in turn seduced the dragon who promptly fell asleep. Jason returned home with the Golden Fleece, and with Medea.

All's well that ends well? No, for King Pelias broke his promise and chased Jason and his bride out of town. Jason himself then broke his marriage promise to Medea and ran off with another girl. Medea, ticked off and jealous, poisoned her rival and disappeared with a carriage drawn by another dragon. Jason was left empty-handed. He fell asleep under his upside-down boat and was crushed when the ship collapsed.

Stories like these, thousands of years old, are origin stories, myths of birth, death and rebirth, of quests, a beginning, an end and a new beginning. Trees that reach toward the sky often play a role: the Golden Fleece in the tree, Anatolian god Attis ending up dead in a tree before being brought back to life, Eve plucking an apple from the tree, Aphrodite's lover Adonis being born from a myrtle branch. The Egyptian god Osiris is cut to pieces by his brother but ends up in a tree where his beloved Isis breathes new life into him. Christ is nailed to the wood and then rises again.

And there is gold everywhere. In Eve's paradise, "the gold is good," and in four hundred other places in the Bible.[155] The story of Isis and Osiris is told to us in a two-millennia-old book entitled *The Golden Ass*. And then there's also a warning tale on the opposite end of the spectrum when Crassus, the general who crushed brave Spartacus's rebellion, died from boiling hot liquid gold his assassins poured down his throat, or at least that's what we are told. These stories are as old as gold itself, and they have been told worldwide.

According to Chinese lore, a golden frog with three legs lives on the moon. The T'ang peaches of immortality are made of gold, "as big as goose eggs." And always there is a golden dragon somewhere that should bring prosperity and health, but fails the job. Japan celebrates the triumphant adventures of Kintaro, the golden boy from the mountains, raised by a woman who eerily resembles Iceland's mountain witch, who gives him only a bib to wear with the word Gold on it. And

Hindu mythology in India warns us not to strip the deity Kuberu of his gold, for gold is the soul of the world.

Gold, in other words, comes with one big warning label: like the first knife, it may cut both ways. Be careful what you wish for. It shines like a new morning, it tempts, it may make you feel wishful, hopeful even, but buyer beware. Yesterday it was a power-hungry, wishful thinking young mythological Greek who shot for the stars but overreached, tomorrow it could be any of us. Gold teaches us to apply our optimism wisely, and to not cease being a realist too.

***

But it is hard to blame humanity for being fascinated. What has fired the imagination of our ancestors for six thousand years is how difficult it always has been to mine the gold. Asks the folks who have been trying to pan some in the Gold Brook bedding in Maine's Franklin and Somerset counties, or in the east branch of Swift River: a speck of gold of a few millimeters at best, if you're lucky. And that's stream bedding prospecting.[156] In South Africa, long the world's main gold producer, a rule of thumb was that in order to mine a ton of gold, 150,000 tons of soil and rock first had to be removed. From shafts that sometimes reached four kilometers deep. Thirty grams of gold, one ounce, as a general principle, required 38 man hours, 1,200 gallons of water, enough electricity to provide light for a family home for 10 days, all in a temperature that could exceed 120 degrees.[157]

Despite all that, it was and is worth it, because of the market price: in 2022, the price of one gram of gold fluctuated all year around fifty dollars. But it comes at the cost of a mountain of effort. And occasionally of an acute emergency. Late 2021, in the Ecuadorian province of El Oro, which means Gold in Spanish, in the community of Zaruma part of downtown suddenly caved. A large, deep sinkhole appeared into which entire houses disappeared. Cause: illegal mining tunnels. Ecuador produces high quality gold largely free of grit and other clinging rock units that is chipped from the Andean mountain strata. This has been done since long before the Incas moved in, and they arrived in the fifteenth century. More than a thousand years of clawing and digging underground finally put Zaruma in a state of emergency.[158]

In short, the bar for bringing out gold sits high. It takes a lot of sweat and sacrifice, and that's what makes it special. But there is more to it than that alone. Gold and everything else that appeals to us because it shines reminds us of an essential need for life. Water. The shiny surface of a brook, a lake, a river, the ocean. Scientists have conducted all kinds of studies about humanity's preference for shiny objects, and in one of them they blindfolded their test participants.[159] They gave them a sheet of glossy paper to feel and asked them to guess what image it showed. All said, "landscapes with water in them".

So, yes, gold has always made many people eager, perhaps not greedy, but yearning, without realizing that they are also reminded of how much they crave the bare essential of water. It was never because they realistically hoped for a life as eternal as their piece of gold, although, you never know, life does maybe get a little easier in the possession of something so valuable. After all, maybe the value only increases. Or you're going to own even more gold. It's akin to what the lottery is today: it contributes to optimism. But when asked point blank, you'll readily admit that it could also very well be wishful thinking.

However, wishful thinking is not the answer you would have heard a century and a half ago if you had asked someone in Colorado, California or the Klondike. Usually men but often enough also women and children were sitting at the bank of a river or stream scooping sand and gravel out of the water with a sieve, hoping to find grains of gold. This was then the modern form of gold prospecting. In Greece three thousand years earlier, the idea of a golden fleece was not a fantasy. Greeks stood or sat beside the water coming down from the mountains, sifting it with a sheepskin. If there was any gold, it would stick in the wool. The sieve used during the Gold Rush was its innovative version.

An estimated three hundred thousand people came flocking from everywhere, first to California. Wishful thinkers? Gold was actually found, so when asked, seekers would say they were being realistic. They had made trips of hundreds and sometimes several thousands of miles for it. But in reality, few got rich. Those who earned good money were mostly merchants, guys who sold coffee, shoes, clothing, tents and blankets to prospectors. Mining the miners, was the common expression, and for a time they were the ones who had every reason for optimism.

Comedian Will Rogers took a look around the Klondike in 1935 and came away shaking his head. He was on his way to Barrow in Alaska, that northernmost town of the world, with a companion who had built his own airplane. They tested if there was a quick and inexpensive way to get mail from California to Russia, via Alaska. Gold prospecting was no answer to "quick and inexpensive," Rogers noticed. "There's a big difference between prospecting for gold and prospecting for spinach," he dictated to the newspapers that ran his syndicated column.

Those were his final printed words. At Barrow, the plane suffered an engine failure and crashed into the water. Both occupants drowned.

Outside Barrow's airport is a monument for Will Rogers. I went and tipped my hat there. I respect people who pursue happiness, whether it's spinach or a new frontier, or simply the shiny water that we cannot do without.

Chapter 20

The benefit of doubt

The vicious pessimism of conspiracy thinking

What about all those weirdos? The ones who say they're convinced that the government plants a mini-chip in someone's arm with every Covid vaccination? Or the ones who hung around Dealey Plaza in Dallas for weeks, waiting for president Kennedy's return? And not only that, they thought John junior would come back, too. And that he would become vice president of the United States, under Donald Trump who would be declared the winner of the 2020 election after all. They waved flags with a big Q, indicating that they counted themselves among a movement started in some remote corner of the deep web by someone who faked having a Q clearance. That's a government term. Anyone with a real security clearance in the Q category has access to top secrets.

One of the most vicious expressions of pessimism is social pessimism, a belief in conspiracies. Such pessimism is almost always a reaction to fear in a world that is coming at the pessimist, a world that is changing too fast for them. It is an expression of dreading an impending but yet invisible doom. This type of anxiety requires a bogeyman. If they cannot be found right away, they are assumed. And then it's seldom limited to one bugaboo, there are more, and they have a plan, a complot, they conspire.

It is of all times, there is indeed nothing new under the sun. Master builder Nehemiah who was commissioned to rebuild the walls of Jerusalem was suspected, according to the Bible story, of carrying out a conspiracy. His defense still stands two thousand years later: "What you say is not true. You made it all up yourself."[160] So, no, complot thinking did not start after JFK's assassination with the rumor that the president had been the victim of a conspiracy. Or with Elvis Presley who, according to more than just a few, is still alive today. As the first Puritans were approaching the Massachusetts shore in 1620, they saw a conspiracy on the horizon. They were coming to bring the true faith, and they didn't doubt for a moment that the devil was waiting for them. He took the form of Indian tribes, the Pequots, the Narragansetts, the Wampanoags. Governor John Winthrop ordered his men to make short work of the conspirators, without mercy.

Therefore, when Edgar Welch from North Carolina stormed into the Comet Ping Pong pizzeria in Washington with an AR-15 assault rifle just before Christmas in 2016 and started shooting the place up, it was by no means the first time a conspiracy theorist had used force. Welch had been told that sex slave trafficking, the selling of young children, was taking place in the pizzeria's pantry and that prominent politicians were behind it, all of whom were pedophiles. This freak theory became since known as Pizzagate, and no one was hurt. Edgar went to prison for four years.

Complot pessimism imagines that others are secretly conspiring for the sake of acquiring or maintaining power and wealth, at the expense of you, your family and your friends. And that nothing will be done about it. But they won't fool you. For you have them in your sights. Like those two hundred dubious women in and around the town of Salem, Massachusetts, witches one and all, handmaidens of the devil. Finally, in 1692, they were dragged to court, twenty were hanged, and that's how their complot was broken up. But what if you, the conspiracy pessimist, had not sounded the alarm?

The fact that such conspiracies at hindsight turn out to have never existed at all is usually no reason to look more critically at the next complot theory. The Salem witches had nothing to do with witchcraft, and their relatives received an apology and compensation afterwards. But that did not stop others from soon seeing new conspiracies, among Masons, Catholics, slaveholders, slave emancipators, white, colored.

Some conspiracy theorists started their own political party. That was the American Party around the mid-nineteenth century, better known as the Know-Nothings, because if anyone asked you if you were a member, you had to say, "I know nothing." After all, those foreign immigrants who were flooding America in the nineteenth century, who were no doubt conspiring to change everything, it was best to not make them any wiser. This didn't stop party members from making very clear where they stood. Swiss Jesuit priest John Pabst who, after learning the Penobscot Nation's language and preaching to them, found himself tarred, feathered and kicked out of town in Ellsworth in 1854, compliments of a mob of Maine Know-Nothings.

And it was not always fringe figures who saw ghosts. Thomas Jefferson wrote, "Single acts of tyranny may be ascribed to the accidental opinion of a day; but a series of oppressions, pursued unalterably through every change of ministers, too plainly prove a deliberate and systematical plan of reducing us to slavery."[161] He saw a conspiracy in England, deliberate and systematic. Eventually, everyone in America, white and black, was going to be turned into a slave by King George III.

Jefferson's language struck a chord, the neighbors believed it, and so did their neighbors.

When prominents join the complot chorus and become lead theorists, it tends to spell trouble. After the Japanese attack on Pearl Harbor, it was a future U.S. Supreme Court Chief Justice who saw a conspiracy, one that should be obvious to everyone, he said. "To assume that the enemy has not planned fifth column activities for us, in a wave of sabotage, is simply to live in a fool's paradise."[162] That was Earl Warren in 1942, then running for governor of California. He called for Japanese immigrant families to be locked up in camps, which subsequently happened. Ten such camps were set up, and over a three-year period, well over a hundred thousand innocent Americans disappeared behind barbed wire.[163]

Less than a decade after Japanese Americans were made to suffer, a new target was invented. "In my opinion," crowed Wisconsin senator Joseph McCarthy from behind a microphone, "the State Department is infested with communists." He waved a sheet of paper. "I have here in my hand a list of 205—a list of names that were made known to the Secretary of State as being members of the Communist Party and who nevertheless are still working and shaping policy in the State Department."[164]

No such list existed, but McCarthy had done his homework. He knew about Samuel Morse's father, the man who had alerted his son that his wife had died. Jedidiah Morse of Connecticut claimed at a separate occasion to have hunted down the Illuminati, an initially Bavarian offshoot of the Masonic order. They were behind the French Revolution, people whispered, and now they were coming to stir up trouble in America as well. "I now have in my possession complete and indisputable proof, an official, authenticated list of the names, ages, places of nativity and professions of the officers and members of a society of Illuminati."[165] Raised index finger and all. President John Adams believed him and declared that the United States was "in a hazardous and afflictive position."[166] Congress passed a law authorizing the president to kick foreigners out of the country at his own discretion. The alleged conspirators were never found.

∗∗∗

Parroting each other. Repeating past examples, counting on the likelihood that no one remembers last time. Spreading rumors of election fraud, knowing that there is always someone somewhere who makes a counting error or votes instead of his mother - and then loudly making an incident the norm. Pointing fingers at easily identifiable groups: people with a different skin color, Jews, the Rockefellers and the Rothschilds, refugees, illegal immigrants, all out to force a "new world order" down the throats of an unsuspecting majority. The goal of such a new world order, according to conspiracy thinkers, is to turn the whole world into a dictatorship.

Even America's currency printers became suspect once somebody alleged on the internet that the words *Novus Ordo Seclorum* on the dollar bill translates to "new world order." The text belongs to a poem by Virgil, is two thousand years old, and was added in 1782 to the Great Seal of brand-new America that with its independence had ushered in "a new order of times". Ignorance is essential to getting another person to believe in your conspiracy theory.[167]

So does the world consist of knowers and non-knowers? Where the knowers are the sensible people, and the non-knowers are conspiracy thinkers? No, because none of us knows anything with certainty about tomorrow and all the tomorrows thereafter. We all face the future blindly, and humanity benefits because without uncertainty there would be no optimism, as there would then be no demand for it. Then everything is certain, then all is fixed, and everyone and everything knows what will and will not happen. There is no hope then either, because hope too is rooted in uncertainty. Not-knowing can drive a person to pessimism, but there is another option, and it plays into the hands of conspiracy thinkers.

We are born with the power of doubt. About everything that takes place outside our immediate peripheral vision, we know nothing for certain, but we have the advantage of doubt. Socrates doubted, so did Hannibal before he crossed the Alps, and the apostle Thomas doubted famously. St. Augustine did, and Plato, and Job doubted from sheer pessimism. Doubts about how things will really turn out, about how they will materialize. Doubts about what we can or cannot believe, which is why they express themselves so often in religions. Conspiracy thinkers are first and foremost doubters, but because they need to be sure, they sometimes delude themselves into believing the stupidest things.

Doubt can be used as a powerful weapon. It is a medicine against blindly accepting what another claims or prescribes. Doubt helps anchor one's autonomy; it can make an individual more independent and stronger. Doubt can inspire self-reflection, it can spur us to arrive at independently drawn conclusions. It is one of a child's earliest discoveries once they find reasons to doubt what the elders around them are saying. Followed by another doubt: if I steal a cookie behind mama's back, does God really see that?

This is the kind of doubt that was nurtured by someone like Mark Twain, who all his life could not understand why God allows so much pain. "Nine-tenths of his disease-inventions were intended for the poor, and they get them." And as if that wasn't already "atrociously cruel" enough, the Lord had sleeping sickness delivered in Africa by "his chosen agent, a fly."[168] Twain did not engage in conspiracy thinking. He was a master of doubt thinking. There's a story about Twain coming to Bangor one day in order to discuss the topic of humor with readers. He tells one funny anecdote after another, but nobody in the audience is laughing. Twain fears he has lost his touch, then doubts this could be true. He mingles among the crowd as they leave, and hears a man say to his wife, "That fella was some funny, wasn't he, mother?" She says, "I think he might have been the funniest person I've heard in my life." And the husband says, "I'll tell ya, he was so funny, it was all I could do to keep from laughing." Tough audience, that was all. Mark Twain was right to doubt his first impression.[169]

***

Among philosophers, there has for several thousands of years been a movement they call Skepticism. It basically says that we should simply accept at face value everything we cannot know, mainly for the sake of our own peace of mind. Suspend judgment, is the adage. In the world of conspiracy thinkers, such a thing falls on deaf ears, but among humorists - and Twain belonged to that category - skepticism is a form of livelihood.

Doubt, moreover, can be overcome. Julius Caesar was at odds with fellow rulers of Rome, doubted whether and how to confront them, and cast a die to make the decision. Benjamin Franklin concluded as a teenager that there was a lot not to like about the Christian faith, and he started reading books to confirm his doubts. However, the more he read, the more he began to embrace the faith.[170]

In contrast, there were Carr van Anda's doubts. He was the editor of the New York Times who in the early morning of April 15, 1912 found a press release from White Star Lines on his desk. The owner of the Titanic announced to the world that their brand new ocean liner, reputedly unsinkable, had touched an iceberg and was therefore delayed but would soon arrive in New York, with everybody on board alive and well.

Newspapers around the nation printed the news that day, but not the Times. Van Anda doubted it. He suspected that hitting an iceberg, with its real mass famously hidden below the water surface, would actually do serious damage to a ship, and so he told his newsroom to wait for confirmation, preferably by telegraph directly from the Titanic. That confirmation never came. The New York Times was the first newspaper to tell the world the next morning, early on April 16, that "Titanic sinks four hours after hitting iceberg; 866 rescued by Carpathia, probably 1250 perish". A doubt confirmed.

And then there was Chinese philosopher Wang Chong. He was a very early skeptic, same vintage as Caesar, but on the other side of the globe. Wang was far ahead of his time. He grew up in poverty during the Han dynasty in Shangyu, just below Shanghai. For years, he spent his days standing between two book stalls, reading manuscripts. The more he learned, the more he doubted. Doubts about thunderstorms that he believed were not punishment from the gods. About the universe of which, according to Wang, there was only one thing to know, which was that no one knew nor could know anything about it. And above all, he doubted the etiquettes of his society. No one, he felt, was entitled to awe and admiration merely because they were rich or had inherited a position of weight. He was what today we would call a healthy skeptic.

For, no, ghosts do not exist, he declared in a society that firmly believed in the spirits of the departed. If they exist at all, Wang said, they have nothing to do with dead people. Since there are far more dead than living, the world would have become overpopulated with ghosts by now, that's why. Clear thinking, two millennia ago, but for the record, Wang Chong added, he was willing to overcome his doubts. He considered it impossible, for example, that humans could ever fly. But he would immediately revise his opinion, he promised, once he saw evidence to the contrary.

Wang did not completely rule it out. But he wasn't holding his breath. For he had never seen a baby born with feathers.

Chapter 21

Shit happens

Optimism that builds on hardship

There's a good chance you don't know who Connie Eble is. Born in 1942, she made it to college professor at a young age. First in Kentucky, then at the University of North Carolina at Chapel Hill. Connie Clare Eble is a linguist who taught English grammar for a long time. She has published all sorts of things, but the only two words that will stick to her for the rest of time are *Shit happens*.

She didn't even come up with them herself. Connie edited an annual publication about college lingo, slang that students use around each other. Each year she asked her students to write their most commonly used expressions on index cards and turn them in to her. In 1983, a young student handed her the words, "Shit happens." The clarification she gave with it was that another student told her he had failed an exam, but he did not let it discourage him. "That shit happens," he said, shrugging his shoulders. Whether this was the very first time anyone had ever used those words is unknown. But Professor Eble's 1983 volume of UNC-CH Slang was the first time it appeared in print.[171] From there, it took on a life of its own.

Mainly because everyone knows it's true, for as long as there have been humans. You can't escape trouble, or what we perceive as trouble. Such as the fact that we will die someday, every one of us. Even Walt Disney. Four newspapers claimed after his death in 1966 that he was only sleeping, like Sleeping Beauty and Snow White, but frozen, in a cylinder.[172] A few weeks later, all the Disney studio heads were called together, to watch a screen. On it, the boss appeared and addressed each of those present individually, by their names. He told them about upcoming projects, flashed a smile, and said he would see them again soon. All for effect, intended for publicity. In reality, chain-smoking Walt Disney was very dead, and he had not selected frost, but fire. His ashes rest in a stone wall at a California cemetery.

Everyone's predictable death could be reason enough for a lifetime of pessimism. But that's not how it works in that 10,000-year-old big brain of ours that allowed us to improve our thinking. Dying falls into the category of *Shit happens.* Just like war, hurricanes, disease and episodes of lack of money. One day they happen. Rising sea levels as the climate continues to warm. Tears when a pet dies. Bitter tears when a loved one passes away. Menopause, waking up sweating in the middle of the night. An astronaut who doesn't return alive. We know this, it is predictable, one day each of us realizes that life sometimes equals suffering.

But we don't become despondent over it. On the contrary, we become resourceful. As humanity became better and more broadly aware of what can go wrong in life, and everyone nonetheless refused to let go of our innate optimism, a new profession popped up in just about every culture. This text, for example, was drafted in the year 1397, in Pisa: "...against acts of God, the sea, nations, fire, and of jettison; of restraint of princes or of peoples or of any other person, of reprisals, of arrest and of every other case, peril, fortune, impediment or mishap, which in any way can happen or may have happened, no matter how or under what condition the cases occur, excepting ballast and custom-house duties."[173] An insurance policy. Humanity began to insure itself against the outbreak of trouble. In and around cities like Genoa, Rome and Venice, it was normal for merchant shipping along the shores of the Mediterranean to insure against shipwreck, spoiled cargo, and pirates.

And not just since the fourteenth century. Insurance policies have been found, carved into basalt, dating back nearly four thousand years to the days of King Hammurabi in Babylonia. Merchants were insured against force majeure. The next step was that governments also insured themselves. Against bad luck, natural disasters, economic setbacks, and also against other governments.

The American War of Independence was fully insured against damage on either side. In Boston, New York and Baltimore there were plenty of underwriters willing to insure the eventuality of war damage on land and sea, out of patriotism and with an eye to self-interest: doing business without having to pay English taxes was going to be a lot more lucrative. In London, the same approach was popular for a while. In Edward Lloyd's former coffee house, agents were initially optimistic about the imminent defeat of the rebellious colony across the Atlantic. The English government could buy policies for a pittance. Until it became clear that America could fight. Then Lloyd's premiums skyrocketed.[174]

* * *

Insurance has only one overall optimistic objective: to collectively bear the risk of the individual, or a group of individuals. If one person is unlucky, she can be reimbursed for her entire loss in exchange for premium payments far below her claim amount. The underwriter's risk is covered because many others also take out such insurance and pay their premiums, even if they themselves never suffer a loss. In effect, they all offset the amount paid out to the one unlucky person, secure in the comforting knowledge that if a covered misfortune should strike them, they too are indemnified. The insurer meanwhile profits, handsomely.

This attitude underscores two things. One: the prediction of hardship does not discourage, but makes creative. Two: hardship does not affect everyone equally, let alone inevitably. Death is inevitable, perishing in a head-on collision is not. Hurricanes happen, but war is avoidable. This is a crucial ingredient of optimism. To aerospace engineer Edward Murphy is invariably attributed the statement that "anything that can go wrong will go wrong at some point," but Ed was in reality an optimist.

He figured that with tests he could determine how much gravitational pressure the human body could withstand and that with this knowledge an astronaut could be hurled into space safely. Most successful laboratory tests are the end result of countless, often intentional, misses and failures. Murphy wanted to know what could go wrong and he let it happen. Eventually, thanks to him, a spacesuit was designed that allowed Alan Shepard, John Glenn and everyone else to escape our atmosphere. Murphy's Law, to Major Murphy's dismay often quoted as an ultimate expression of pessimism, was born out of optimism.

If every woe were inevitable, ten millennia ago optimism would have been a stillborn child. But the ancient grandfathers and grandmothers soon discovered that much calamity was preventable, and their first case in point was the cooking pot. They had finally managed to prevent their toothless children from starving to death. Even better, now that everyone could be served soft meals, they at least got their vitamins and therefore, over time, fewer teeth fell out.

It took time for humanity's brain pan to grow to its current dimensions, but the ancestors gradually learned from bad news after it had already hit them once. As we saw earlier, people spend a huge amount of time daydreaming. Part of that is the reenactment of choices made earlier, reactions to events that happened prior. One of its effects is the phenomenon of a forewarned man, of the fox and the snare. What went wrong last time may be avoidable next time. That's how hope began to triumph over experience.

Moreover, people are very skilled at compartmentalizing everything their big brain registers. They can separate feelings and temporarily push them aside. This prevents getting overwhelmed by worries about tomorrow. And most of all, it avoids becoming paralyzed by the knowledge that one day there is going to be an inevitable end to our existence. Instead, we are skilled at focusing on all the threats, dangers, woes, sorrows, natural disasters, illness and pain that can one day be made avoidable without debilitating us emotionally.

In addition, the ancestors discovered something else. They lived close to nature and saw an essential difference between themselves and all other mammals. Humans are capable of imitating each other. Not in the way father eagle teaches his chicks to fly, or mother whale who shows her calves how to negotiate shallow water. People can imitate other people's inventions with their heads and hands, and what's more, they can improve on them. After Grandma Van Cleve's grandsons Wilbur and Orville Wright invented the airplane, Anthony Fokker could do it too, and better.[175] After him, Conrad Westervelt turned it into a seaplane, along with his buddy William Boeing, whereupon Victor Roos, like the Wright brothers a bicycle mechanic, managed to design a cheap Cessna. All a matter of imitation and improvement.

Modern societies temporarily protect their inventors from imitation by granting patents, but these only confirm the unique biological and anthropological reality underlying them. We can do what others can do, and soon can do it better. Thus, for ten thousand years, man has been learning, step by step, to overcome inevitabilities until they are no longer inevitable.

***

Humanity has in fact succeeded beyond all expectations. In the year 1798, British economist Robert Malthus expressed concern about the world's population, which around that time was estimated to be a billion men and women. That was an overpopulation, he warned. It was the result of better food, which was a result of better agricultural methods. Malthus welcomed those improvements, but he nevertheless called them a trap, since known as the *Malthusian trap*.[176] It is absolutely impossible, he warned, that the Earth can sustain so many people in the long run: "The power of population is so superior to the power of the Earth to produce subsistence for man, that premature death must in some shape or other visit the human race." In other words, the power of sex was considered stronger than the power of imagining that our species could, over time, resolve the dilemma.

We are now two centuries further in time. One hundred years after Malthus, the world housed twice as many inhabitants. By 1960 the count was 3 billion, 15 years later 4 billion, 12 years after that 5 billion, 6 billion in the year 2000, and 7 billion in 2010.[177] Such figures indicate two parallel phenomena. One: the Earth is capable of providing much more nourishment than pessimist Malthus assumed, and two: people did not die prematurely. On the contrary, their average life expectancy went up by leaps and bounds. This was in large part due to revolutionary changes in farming that the economist had not seen coming.

At the time Robert Malthus wrote down his essay "On the Principle of Population," ninety percent of the American population lived and worked on farms. Today this is a mere one percent. Back then, one farmer produced food that was enough to keep three to five people alive for a year. Today's farmer feeds 130 people.[178] And that's in the relatively old-fashioned way: farm, field, barns, pasture, tractors. It can be done much better.

Because if you want to understand why optimism is truly appropriate when it comes to where the world's food production is headed, again, you can't ignore the example of the Dutch. If you follow the day-to-day news, you can't always tell, because there you'll find big headlines about problems, about angry farmers, questions about manure management and nitrogen. All relevant, and all true, but it also masks a very different story, an improbable success tale of innovation.

The Dutch agribusiness decided a quarter century ago, in consultation with their government, to go all in on that path of innovation so that food production can be guaranteed for a world population that will reach ten billion sometime between 2050 and 2060, while at the same time using less water and making the environment cleaner. In other words, how to make agriculture more sustainable, faster. Or as the Dutch described it, "Produce twice as much food with twice as few resources." Dutch farmers have succeeded in reducing the amount of water they need for most crops by 90 percent. They no longer use pesticides at all in their greenhouses, and the use of antibiotics on chicken and cattle farms has been cut in half.

After all, in the coming decades, the world must produce more food than all farmers combined have harvested in the past 8,000 years. Stop and think about that for a moment. Go back twenty, thirty years in time, and ask yourself then, when you were that much younger, if you would find it realistic and believable that during the rest of your lifetime this would be achievable. This being: increase all the world's harvests to such a level that it exceeds all the food that our forebears together have harvested since six thousand years before the day Christ was born.

Maybe you would have said yes, but there would have been others who would have strongly doubted it. Those would have called you an optimist, and that's exactly what those ambitious planners were and are. They realized that this production increase is what it will take to feed all those new mouths by mid-century. And they decided it is possible - provided it's done smartly. Today, their farmers are already the largest exporters of potatoes, and they are using farming equipment that looks like it came straight out of Star Trek to tend to their spuds until they can be harvested.

Harvesters are equipped with cockpit-like instruments that track data collected by drones that let them know exactly, for each individual potato, how soil chemistry, water and nutrients are doing. That way they can see at a glance how far this particular one tuber has grown. The term they use for this is precision farming, and such precision yields them 50 tons of potatoes per acre. The average yield in the rest of the world is twenty-two tons per acre, less than half.[179]

Think outside the box, stop growing endless fields of grain or soy for animal feed. Rather feed your livestock insects, they say at Wageningen University, the world's leading agro-science center. The same two acres that provide one ton of soy protein a year produce 150 tons of insect protein. Innovate, try new things: Dutch farmers have become the world's largest tomato exporters, using greenhouses that cover an area nearly twice the size of Manhattan to save energy and water. While U.S. farmers need 14 gallons of water to grow one pound of tomatoes, the Dutch use barely one gallon, just rainwater, and no soil. The plants grow nearly seven feet tall and root in fibers made of basalt and lime, and a constant ambient temperature is guaranteed year-round with geothermal heat from aquifers deep beneath the Dutch soil.

Good news: famines are becoming scarce.[180] One hundred years ago, sixteen million people died of starvation, mostly in China and in what was then the young Soviet Union. By 1960 the number was still that high, over sixteen million, mainly because Mao's Great Leap Forward in China did not work out as advertised. But the number of starvation deaths declined rapidly after that, from three million in the 1970s, half of them in Cambodia, to less than three million in the first decade of the new millennium, to less than 300,000 in the six years after that.

It is the result of a better and more efficient food production, which means that more food is available per person. This is particularly true in India and China, the two countries where in the past 150 years half of all starvation deaths have occurred. Overall health worldwide has also improved dramatically, while at the same time the worst poverty has declined, again especially in China and India, home to 40 percent of the world's population. These factors combined have had another important effect: women worldwide are having fewer children than before.

Healthier people with better access to cleaner water are more likely to escape extreme poverty. They are also more likely to go to school, which in turn affects the number of offspring as more and more of those students are female. Women with a college education keep family sizes down. Famine mainly affects children under five. As the number of new babies decreases, so does the number of people dying of starvation. Add it all up, and you are looking at "one of the great under-reported victories of our time," said British social anthropologist, Harvard and Tufts professor and Africa expert Alex de Waal.[181]

The Dutch effort is in part a response to a dark episode in their own recent past. The last time a serious famine hit a Western country occurred during the closing winter of World War II, in Holland. The country's largest population centers were cut off from food supplies and twenty thousand Dutch men, women and children starved to death. This was partly a Nazi revenge after the failed Allied attempt in 1944 to capture a bridge across the Rhine at Arnhem, but also a result of an unusually long and cold winter that made food shipments by water impossible.

Therefore the generations since then have been doing everything they can to prevent this from recurring, and to help others. For example, by improving soil quality control. There are 570 million farms around the world, and only five percent have access to scientific data about their soils.[182] The Dutch invented a phone app, along with a scanner, to show a farmer in Kenya in ten minutes how to change the composition of his fertilizer and nutrients to get higher yields. They figured out how to grow more tomatoes, peppers, cucumbers and eggplants by fertilizing them with fish waste, from which they extracted the ammonia to make nitrate with which to water the plants.

They refined water culture, acquired a patent for a rotary milking machine that allows one person to milk 150 cows in an hour, and they made their greenhouses almost entirely disease-free, protected by hunting mites, the larvae of ladybugs and tiny worms that mushrooms crave. Holland, with an area that is one-ten thousandth of all the land on Earth, is now the world's second-largest food exporter, after the U.S., and supplies the rest of the world with one-third of all food seeds, without genetic manipulation. One tomato seed from Holland is capable of naturally defending itself against disease and, to boot, of providing 150 tons of tomatoes. And none of this is knowledge the Dutch keep to themselves.

They are working with Ethiopia to improve the quality of potatoes there, with China to transport produce fresh and safely in a train container between Rotterdam and Chongquing, with Kazakhstan to develop rubber from the roots of dandelions, with Indonesia to prevent the loss of even more forest to encroaching farming, with Ghana to make their vegetable market sustainable, with India to reduce water use in rice cultivation. And so on.

Shit happens. But it is less and less often inevitable. Because it inspires optimists to find solutions, and if one small country can pull this off, wait until others follow the example. We ain't seen nothing yet.

Chapter 22

The single men and women of Russia and China

When optimism triumphs over making babies

Japan sells more diapers for the elderly than for babies. In the United States there are more grandparents than grandchildren. And Siberia counts so many unmarried women that they're having an active debate about allowing polygamy: "Half a good man is better than no man."[183] At first glance, you would think that neighboring China, with a surplus of 35 million men, could provide a reservoir of candidates. But other than single women, Siberia doesn't have much to offer. It is barren, empty, cold and in many ways unwelcoming. Eighty percent of all 145 million Russians live on the other side of the Ural Mountains, sitting on twenty percent of all available Russian land. They are aging. Not yet as bad as in Japan, but there are more Russians over forty than under, and that's saying something in a country where men on average do not even reach the age of 65.[184]

China's dimensions add up to only half the size of Russia. But China counts ten times as many people. And here, too, the land is unevenly populated. The country has a large central plain, where roughly four thousand years ago the origins of China began. One billion Chinese live there, one thousand million, seventy percent of the entire population. The area is half the size of the U.S., and America has a much smaller population, 330 million. It is also heavily polluted. At times, the Yellow River literally looks yellow from the waste that makes its way to the ocean across a distance of three thousand miles.

China is paying a price for years of limiting family size. Compared to just twenty years ago, it has 90 million fewer residents in the 15-35 age group, and 150 million more people over 60.[185] This is not just the result of the one-child rule that was in place between 1980 and 2015.[186] Even before then, Chinese couples were already cutting back on family size, especially in and around cities.[187] Almost as if all people, everywhere, are biologically wired to recognize when reproduction needs to take a step back. For it is clear that the urge to reduce the number of children has become a noticeable phenomenon worldwide, east, west, north and south.

In Singapore, this is a concern for its government. Young people are getting married alright, with husband and wife both working for the five Cs: cash, car, credit card, country club and a condo. But having children is being procrastinated. A decade ago, the government therefore decided to send a letter to young childless couples, encouraging them to start a family. They were even offered a special date: the night of Aug. 9, 2012, "National Night."[188] Singapore added its reason: to secure the community's strong economy for the long term, more kids are necessary, enough young people who will soon be able to assure retirement and health care for the elderly.

The government added a bonus, a free vacation in Bali. There, they reasoned, young couples would naturally get into the right mood.

Sure enough, many couples eagerly accepted the offer. But whatever it was that they did during their free vacation, it did not cause any additional pregnancies, and neither did National Night. The government ended the bonus program after nine months.

***

The effects of a slowed-down population growth vary from country to country, but the deeper cause had been manifesting itself for some time. From three billion people on Earth in 1960 to eight billion within seventy years is a pace that, if left unchecked, is going to be seriously problematic to sustain, one that begs to be slowed down, even if it comes with all kinds of socioeconomic consequences in the short term. Clearly, even without one-child laws, and also without necessarily looking at the wider perspective, humanity intuitively recognizes that from time to time there are limits to growth that need to be observed.

In this book's earlier chapter about knives and table manners we looked at what it meant, eight billion people on Earth by the year 2030. As we saw, well-sourced estimates show that, since the birth of homo sapiens two hundred thousand years ago, roughly 110 billion births and deaths preceded us. That's an average of 1.1 billion people in every two thousand years, 500 million per millennium, fifty million births per century, 1,400 new babies per day. Today, twice that many children are born every ten minutes. They arrive in a world that, if carefully distributed through the modern logistics now available, and if growth is checked, has enough to eat and drink for them.

But averages don't mean much for those looking at making a snapshot here and there. Humanity has had narrow escapes a few times. Pandemics have decimated entire peoples. Climate changes, mainly bitter cold waves, nearly ended the phenomenal adventure of humans on Earth.[189] For a while, of every hundred men and women and children, when trying to flee from the cold, five, six at most, survived. Plagues, smallpox, war, fevers, diarrhea and, most recently, mass outbreaks of influenza have since been the main culprits for grotesque numbers of casualties.

All the more remarkable is the recent explosive growth of the world population, especially since the dawn of the previous century. Even more so against the backdrop of the first half of that century, when two world wars, an unprecedented global economic depression and the Spanish flu outbreak caused a staggering number of deaths. Better nutrition, cleaner water, better education for many more girls, more prosperity, better lines of communication, cheaper transportation, faster communication and the elimination of many diseases: all of this combined has made room for more people with a higher and more comfortable life expectancy.

But even that is only a snapshot in time. For the future has only just begun. After all, if our species is indeed two hundred thousand years old, biologists will instead say, two hundred thousand years *young*. The average mammal species, so far, has had an estimated lifespan of one million years. We humans are only one-fifth down that stretch. Compare this to an average human life that today spans eighty years, and you'll note that we as a species are currently only sixteen years old. Humanity still has eight hundred thousand years ahead of us.

What does this mean for all those who will come after us? How many will there be? Can the planet handle that? So far, 110 billion people, plus our eight billion today, have lived on and off the face of the Earth. If everyone after us averages not eighty but at least ninety years of age, which is not an unreasonable assumption, and the world population stagnates at eleven billion, which is the number that the United Nations predicts for 2099, then 100 trillion children will be born after us. That's 1 with fourteen zeros. By comparison, all babies born to date since the biological Adam and Eve add up to 1 with eleven zeros.

But we know nothing for certain about the future average lifespan of men and women. Maybe they will get to reach a much older age. And it is entirely possible that there could be many more than 11 billion people living on Earth at any given period of time. Moreover, it is in no way set in stone that the human mammal can survive only a million years. It could just as easily be a billion years, who knows, or five billion, which is as long as the sun is projected to last. If all of the above were to come true, the estimated number of babies that will have to live on and off the earth in the future increases massively. The analysts at Oxford University say 625 quadrillion. That's 625 followed by fifteen zeros.

How much is that? Suppose you give one man or woman their own little patch of beach, small, ten square feet. They can only stand or sit, arms wrapped around their knees. In your mind, make that beach six yards wide, so that between the boardwalk and the water six people are forming a line, each sitting or standing on their own ten square feet. Next to them there's another line of six men and women, and next to them also, and so on. That six-yard-wide beach runs from Barrow in the extreme north of Alaska all the way to Ushuaia in the far south of Argentina. Correct, that's the same distance I traveled by helicopter, the full length of the Pacific beach from Arctic Circle to Antarctic Circle. That's 625 trillion people.

***

These kinds of estimates assume that we'll not prematurely be blowing ourselves up already. For the first time in history, we can do that - there are, and have been for seventy years, more than enough nuclear warheads kept in arsenals to kill all life on Earth. That alone is reason enough for a high state of vigilance, but there is more that demands our attention. More than a few countries have kept samples of every deadly disease that has since been eradicated, often in military laboratories.

I lived for twenty years about a mile from Fort Detrick in Maryland. It is the headquarters of what is identified as the United States Army Medical Research Institute of Infectious Diseases (USAMRIID), in short, a biodefense army post. It's where the U.S. government prepares for defending against biological warfare attacks. Every night at ten I heard from my house a trumpet playing taps at Fort Detrick.

The 1996 film *Outbreak*, starring Dustin Hoffman, Renee Russo and Morgan Freeman, was about a military virus laboratory from where Ebola spores escaped. Fort Detrick was the model for that fictional story, and correctly so, because five years later, nonfictionally, real-life anthrax was stolen there. Shortly after the September 11, 2001 terrorist attacks, a mad Detrick scientist mailed letters containing anthrax around the country, which resulted in five deaths. The perpetrator lived next door to the camp, and initially volunteered helping the police search for the origin of the mailed anthrax. Eventually, after the FBI realized who they were working with, the man committed suicide.

In other words, countries that talk the talk about proliferation and non-proliferation of nuclear weapons could also be more careful about protecting their citizens from mass disease outbreaks. In October 1977, the World Health Organization reported that after three thousand years smallpox was officially eradicated. A patient in Somalia was the last one known to be infected, he had been successfully treated, and everyone who had been in contact with him had been vaccinated. Nevertheless, ten months later in the English city of Birmingham a new infection occurred.

The victim worked as a photographer in the same building that also housed a smallpox laboratory on a different floor. The virus had escaped. The patient got sick, as did her parents, father died from a heart attack, the lab owner committed suicide, and the accidentally infected woman died of smallpox on September 11, 1978. So far at least, she is considered the very last smallpox victim.[190]

It is all avoidable. No matter how far into the future we look, massive nuclear and/or infectious disasters are not inevitable. They are possible, perhaps even probable, but not inevitable. One hundred billion new people, one hundred trillion or even one hundred quadrillion - these are just as many walking risks, but they are also just as many new talents, people with brilliant brains and intuitions, global citizens with ideas and solutions to problems whose future existence we cannot even imagine today.

***

Edward Murphy, the aerospace engineer, has been rumored to have come up with another statement beside Murphy's Law that said everything that can go wrong, will go wrong. The other one reads: everything that can happen, will one day happen. Ed later insisted he never used those words either, but they are seductive in their simplicity. As if the world were a roulette: one day the ball will fall into the pocket, it's a matter of time, a matter of waiting for it to happen. Inevitably.

But Croatian Frano Selak, in January 1962, was on a train that derailed and fell into a river, and he suffered only a broken arm and a wet suit. Seventeen others drowned. The following year he traveled for the first time in an airplane. It too ran into trouble. The door flew open, Frano fell out and landed in a haystack. His nineteen fellow passengers crashed and died. In 1966, he was on a bus that veered out of control and also fell into a river. Four died, but not Frano, who suffered only minor bruises. Four years later he had a car accident, the gas tank exploded, but not until after Mr. Selak had jumped out. In 1973 something went wrong again, flames shot out of the dashboard while he was driving, but Frano suffered only scorched hair. He was hit by another bus, dodged a truck and slid into a ravine, and finally, after he married for the fifth time, he bought a lottery ticket. Frano Selak won 900,000 dollars.[191]

Some say that his was an example of: everything that can happen, will one day happen. Others look at the same story and conclude that any of those incidents could have ended Selak's life, and that statistically it became more likely by the day, but: it did not happen, it was clearly and obviously not inevitable. On the contrary, the man became rich, bought a boat and then gave away all his money to friends and family. Frano Selak lived to be 87, which was old for his generation.

I have on my bookshelf two books on this subject that have been sitting there for years. I read them when they came out, in 2008 and 2007, respectively, *Outliers* by Malcolm Gladwell and *The Black Swan* by Nassim Nicholas Taleb. It is easy to understand why they both topped the New York Times best-sellers list at the time. Their popularity had a reason. People need confirmation of what they all subconsciously feel and know: improbable things happen despite being improbable. Gladwell and Taleb talked about that. They presented a whole series of examples of coincidences, exceptions to the rule, unexpected discoveries and events. Improbabilities that, when added together, lose their improbability in retrospect.

You can argue back and forth whether or not the September 11, 2001 attack was foreseeable, and whether or not Google became the internet's number one search engine by accident.

You can argue whether or not ten thousand hours of practicing on something makes anyone a potential top-performer. But what the consumer interest in such arguments makes clear is that whether something is probable or improbable does not, on balance, matter to the vast majority of people. People have hope. We are born with optimism. We look continuously for reinforcement of our faith in possibility, our belief in sensing that doomsday is not coming, no matter how loud the predictions to the contrary are that some politicians, pastors and broadcasters keep raining upon us.

Ask people in Russia or China how optimistic they are, knowing that they face challenges about the composition of their populations, and you'll get a surprising answer. The Paris-based research firm Ipsos, London-based YouGov and Pew Research Center in Washington ask that question every year in up to forty countries.[192] Russia is the land with the unfortunate geography. It is so far stretched from west to east that it covers eleven time zones. From the Ural Mountains, a 1200-mile wide plain stretches westward, something that makes Russian rulers permanently nervous because it is flat and therefore, as Napoleon and Hitler demonstrated, crossable. It sometimes makes them do stupid things, like the 2022 invasion of Ukraine, which only made NATO countries more determined to strengthen their alliance. Result: an even more nervous Moscow.

On the other side of the Urals, however, they don't notice much of this. They know from hearsay that Russia broke up into 15 different countries after the dissolution of the Soviet Union, but this didn't affect them all that much. They are happy that party obligations no longer exist, a feeling shared by their compatriots on the other side of the mountains. And when their government suddenly reinstates the military draft, calling up their young men for military service, they understandably protest. Plus there is that issue of Siberian women and the absence of enough eligible men. The girls accuse guys of irresponsibility, mainly because of their drinking habits that have an effect on male mortality rates. But they are not pessimistic. Time and again, surveys show that Russians are more optimistic than Americans, Germans, Dutch, French and the British.[193]

The same is true for Chinese and Indians. They are routinely more optimistic than Americans, Canadians and all of Western Europe. This is all the more telling, given that in all those Western countries, optimism scores high regardless, with three-quarters of the population having a sunny outlook about the future. Seventy-five is a high percentage - but Russians and Chinese score higher yet. The researchers invariably take a look behind the numbers and distinguish between optimism about one's personal life and confidence in the future of their country. Among other things, this shows that for the short term, it makes little difference whether a person lives in a democracy or not. For the future, however, it does make a difference. Indians, who live in a democracy, are then ten percent more optimistic than the Chinese, who do not.

And the Singaporeans? They have a rock-solid confidence in their future despite their government's admonitions. There, as in the U.S., seventy-five percent of citizens give a thumbs-up. And in Turkey, the home country of hearing-impaired Muharrem Yazgan, the man who was suddenly capable of communicating with his neighbors after they started using sign language, just about everyone is full of hope. Almost ninety percent of all Turks say they expect that this future of ours will work out just fine.

Chapter 23

But what about Africa?

How optimism replaces longtime suffering

The very first e-reader to find a market was the Rocket eBook, invented by Marc Tarpenning who later also spearheaded the Tesla. I met Marc at a book festival in Charlottesville, Virginia, in the spring of 2001. He was sitting behind an empty table, holding one of those Rockets, a tablet the size of a thin paperback with a greenish grey screen. He attracted little attention. People who came to a book festival expected to see stacks of books. Marc Tarpenning had also brought a small stack, but they were all hidden behind that screen. Ten books fit into the storage capacity of his Rocket.

He didn't seem very disturbed by the limited attention from festival attendees, nor should he have been. The Rocket eBook product had just been sold for nearly two hundred million dollars to a major publisher, people who, like Marc, understood how vast the future of batteries would be.[194] And sure enough, before the decade was out, the market for electronic books had exploded. Kindle, Apple Books and Kobo are now global house-hold names, and the share of ebooks relative to all books sold has been hovering around 20 percent for some time now.

Everywhere except in Africa where it is much higher, on the continent that for centuries has seemed like it is Mother Nature's stepchild. Africa, where homo sapiens took their first steps, where humanity's great adventure began. And its great journey, too, for it was Africa from where our ancestors began to walk, along the shores of the Mediterranean Sea into Europe, where they drew pretty menu pictures on rock walls. Others walked into Asia, the first to discover how large Siberia is, then crossed into Alaska, before populating the North and South American continents. They did not grow old, they walked step by step, foot by foot, at most a few miles per generation, but they were unstoppable. They were emigrants. From Africa, the cradle of us all.

It is the continent that in many people's minds now con-jures up images of famine, poverty, civil wars and disease. Where only half a century ago people died on average thirty years younger than in the West, where in countries like Kenya and Ghana one in four children did not reach the age of four-teen. It is a picture that needs updating. For although people in Africa still have a shorter life expectancy than elsewhere, those thirty years have now been cut in half. In the same period that in Europe the mortality rate fell by three percent, it improved by 65 percent in Africa.[195] And while infant mortal-ity is still far too high, it no longer affects one in four children, but one in ten.

It has consequences. Africa does not have a problem with aging like China, Japan and Russia. Twice as many children are born here as in China, and ten times as many as in the U.S. More than a billion people live in the 50 countries that make up sub-Saharan Africa, countries not bordering the Mediterra-nean. That number is growing so rapidly that Africa will soon have more people than China and will be second behind India. The United Nations expects Africa to count two billion people before 2040 and then grow to three billion within 20 years.[196]

Africans are getting healthier, they are eating better, women are going to school more often and for longer, and therefore they are living longer. With smaller families than before, but because they are on average reaching a much older age, the population is still growing faster. There is plenty of space. The continent is huge, larger than most maps suggest, and considerably larger than we used to learn in school.

The surface areas of western and eastern Europe fit into it, along with all of China, India and Japan, and still that leaves enough space for all of the U.S. as well. It has plenty and deep river water, and there is so much fertile land that can be made suitable for livestock and agriculture and horticulture, that eight hundred thousand square miles will soon become available for grass and crops. That's an area as large as England, Germany, the Benelux countries, France, Spain and Italy combined.

Much leaves to be desired. Such as access to clean and running water, electricity, hygienic bathrooms - the continent has more cell phones than toilets, as in: way, way more. But therein lies also one of the main causes of Africa's leap forward. The continent is skipping steps. Africans are big cell phones users, ninety percent of the population have one. The telephone era with land lines pretty much passed Africa by; now Africa is skipping land lines. It is much more efficient for telephone companies to erect cell phone towers everywhere than it is to run cables. Marc Tarpenning realized a quarter century ago how great the future would be for powerful batteries, and now Africa more than any other part of the world shows how right he was.

Most payments by phone take place in Africa, mainly because many people do not have traditional bank accounts.

In Kenya, three-quarters of all money transactions go by phone, giving the capital city of Nairobi the nickname Silicon Savannah.[197] Most telephone consultations with doctors and pharmacies: also in Africa.[198] Men and women can now order goods that are not available in the local market. And they can read books.

African families outside major cities have little or no access to bookstores or libraries. But through their phones and, increasingly, their e-readers, they can get their hands on virtually any book they want to read. The spread of information and increase in knowledge in Africa has been nothing short of spectacular since the beginning of this century. And all this adds up to the expectation that Africa is the continent where the next industrial revolution will be taking place.[199]

More agribusiness leads to more demand for more industrial equipment, products manufactured in more new factories. That comes with an increased demand for transportation, and thus the construction or improvement of infrastructures. Slums are being mapped with QR codes, allowing repairs to happen faster and families to finally have a real address where they can receive mail.[200] A farm that no longer only feeds the local population but also has excess production to sell provides more jobs for a processing industry: companies that are canning fruit, bakeries that bake cakes and cookies, dairy that goes to stores in cartons and bottles.

Foreign knowledge imports are helping farmers in Africa to improve their production, particularly of cassava, a root that requires rapid processing in order to make it suitable for food, beer and wood products. The farmer receives cash payment, and does not themselves have to invest in harvesting equipment. Everything is mobile in Africa, the telephone, the library, the doctor, and therefore also the carrot peeler, washer and pulverizer. The mobile machines come and go as needed, and return as soon as the next harvest is ready.[201]

There are ifs and buts. Africa is traditionally politically unstable. Just like that, another dictatorship can break out somewhere, or a bloody civil war, or a conflict between tribes. Lawlessness and anarchy affect half of all African countries from time to time, and people flee from them, usually from rural areas to cities. And although famine has been reduced in just a few years to a mere quarter of what it was, food shortages usually hit Africa first and hardest. Moreover, out of the blue another epidemic can pop up anywhere on the continent. AIDS is a scary example: 36 million deaths worldwide, but two-thirds of all victims were Africans.

Nevertheless, there is more hope today than ever, and all trends point in the right direction. In Africa, as elsewhere in the world, optimism is spreading in particular through women. Better and longer education frees them from marriages at too young an age and pregnancies that come too early and are too frequent, and as a result it is often they who are driving the engine of a new economy. The number of women entrepreneurs in Africa is growing steadily, and this is encouraging more and more other women to seek stable employment.

***

Facebook, LinkedIn, eBay, Google, Tesla and Intel have in common that they were all founded or co-founded by immigrants. In 2020, the U.S. had 87 "unicorn" companies, private businesses worth more than a billion dollars. Half of these, 44 companies, were conceived and founded by immigrants.[202] Roughly 13 percent of all American residents are foreign-born, but of all doctors and surgeons, 28 percent are immigrants, and so are 22 percent of all nurses.[203] Of the 86 American Nobel laureates since 2000 in the categories of chemistry, medicine and physics, 33 were born in another country, nearly 40 percent. And when President Ronald Reagan fell victim to an assassination attempt on March 30, 1981, almost the entire staff in the operating room at George Washington Hospital was foreign-born.[204]

Migrants are optimists, always, even when they are fugitives on a trek to a better country, a better future. Almost without exception, they are hard workers. "Immigration is pure entrepreneurship. You leave behind everything familiar to start somewhere new. To succeed, you need to develop alliances. You must acquire skills. You will have to improvise on occasion. It's a bold proposition," entrepreneur Reid Hoffman said of his colleagues from France, Vietnam and Germany with whom he founded LinkedIn.[205]

Of all the world's migrants, 72 percent are of a working age, compared with 58 percent of the total population. In the U.S., immigrants account for 47 percent of the growth in labor production since 1990. In Europe, it is as much as 70 percent.[206] Their tax payments generously exceed what they collect through social insurance. These are data that shouldn't surprise any of us, because we see its reality around us every day, regardless of where we live. And no matter how often and how loudly groups oppose allowing new migrant flows to cross their borders, it does in the long run not change the principle that where opportunities are available, opportunity seekers will come in. Sometimes it is caused by aging, at other times it's innovation that provides work for new hands, hearts and heads.

It requires fitting in, adapting and adjusting for everyone, but never does resistance last longer than one generation.

Chapter 24

America, the world's captain

The optimism of a new generation

The United States is the only country in the world that is populated by people from every nation in the world. Every language in the world is spoken in the U.S. somewhere at some point, on the street, in a kitchen, in a hospital bed. The country is a magnet. America, fiercely criticized from all sides for her excesses, is for most non-Americans head and shoulders the preeminent symbol of freedom and opportunity.

This has been true since her birth as an independent nation in 1776, but especially after the liberation of four million slaves at the end of the Civil War in 1865, when an explosion of productivity and innovation opened all doors and windows across the continent and let a fresh breeze in. The 1893 World's Expo in Chicago attracted nearly thirty million visitors from forty countries who stared with mouths agape at the latest revolutionary triumphs of technology. And while many of the critical notes are based on hard facts, what stands out above it

all is that in America the critics have every right and freedom
to express them out loud and on the top of their lungs.

America is a land of class-acts and weirdos, of fools and ge-
niuses. A society of cowboys and movies, of guns and the arts,
of awe and scorn. It is a nation of laws and law enforcement.
Everyone is allowed to lie, provided they don't defame and are
not under oath, and all may freely rant against presidents, ex-
presidents, the FBI, the Red Cross and God. They have been
exercising their ranting rights for four hundred years, except
when Peter Stuyvesant and his wooden peg-leg were still in
charge. If you were blasphemous on Sundays, he'd put you
behind bars with his own strong hands.

Without America's liberty, freedom has a scant future.
Without America's openness, innovation and, yes, bellowing
laughter, hope will be in short supply worldwide. This may
be a hard fact to swallow for those who have, while sneering
neener-neener, convinced themselves that the country is on
the edge of a cliff and cannot escape another civil war, but if
America were to fail, much else will fail.

However, this is no longer the decade of 1970s, when a
bomb went off just about every week somewhere in America.
Or the 1960s when white men set fire to a church with impunity, regardless of whether young girls with a different skin
color wearing white dresses were inside choking and burning.
The days when demonstrators against the war in Vietnam were
shot at with live rounds, and when police stood by as clubs
landed on peaceful marchers, men and women who wanted to
be able to send a child to a color-blind school.

A civil war where people are willing to kill their neighbors
involves more than yelling, "Stand back and stand by!" on
Twitter or the deep web. Such hostilities are usually preceded
by a long and deep injustice, often combined with a high
unemployment. By contrast, America in the 2020s is going
through a period of virtually zero unemployment; there are

more jobs than job seekers. And it has no deeper injustice than what some groups have traditionally been suffering. But the cries for civil war are not coming from those corners, not from Black neighborhoods, not from women whose authority over their own bodies has been taken away from them by their governor or state parliament.

America is a nation where men and women under forty are in the majority, with more rich women than rich men.[207] Also a nation where, although there are more sixty-plus seniors than Millennials, a record number of weddings have been taking place lately, more than ever since the early 1980s.[208] Getting married, as we have seen, is a standard expression of optimism, an event for which bride, groom and their parents are happily forking over an average of more than thirty thousand dollars, easily. They do so in a post-pandemic country that offers so many job opportunities that more and more people are wondering how much longer those migrants at the border should be stopped from coming in.

It is the country that wears the world's captain armband, marching down a wide avenue, towards a sunrise, a new day, a tomorrow. Sounds old-school optimistic? It does, rightly so, and I will show you why.

***

The United States, despite the influx of Italian, Irish and German immigration in the second half of the nineteenth century, does not resemble Italy, nor does it mirror Germany. It does not look like Ireland or France. With much good will, you could say it looks a little like England, but that is largely because of the language. However, in that case it increasingly looks just as much like Mexico, Honduras, El Salvador or Venezuela. Immigrants from there are now so numerous that the effect they have on street signage, in stores and on TV is hard to overlook.

America today does however resemble, above all, the nation that founded it, the optimistic people who came sailing from overseas four hundred years ago and who built its early infrastructures. They were America's mother, as the influential grandfather of Maine's folk singer Gordon Bok, The Ladies Home Journal's editor Edward Bok, described them in 1903 to the magazine's two million subscribers.[209] They gave the new land the Knickerbockers, the Roosevelts, the Rockefellers, the Vanderbilts, the Fonda's, the Brando's, the DeNiro's and the Cronkites.[210] You are giving me a puzzled look, but let me draw a picture for you that explains why especially today, in these days of widespread discontent, the comparison holds up.

The reality is that America has become what its Dutch founders, the builders, in the seventeenth century envisioned. It was not founded in order to become a Dutch colony; it was an enterprise, an overseas affiliate. While the Dutch West India Company worked closely with politicians in Amsterdam and The Hague, it was primarily a business, a multinational corporation. New Netherland, across the ocean, was a for-profit business establishment. An ambitious product of what many people at the time felt was an actual golden age of optimism.

Ideally, the merchants of those days would have wanted the Seven United Provinces to be able to maintain their world hegemony indefinitely. But if they could see in person today what has become of their enterprise across the Atlantic, they would say: our seven United Provinces have become fifty United States. The world's unrivaled superpower. Good job. Now where's the infighting?

For those trying to understand why there is so much nagging and nattering going around America, the comparison with four hundred years ago is a surprisingly good and adequate guide. The country is going through what in the Netherlands at the time was known as the Twelve Years' Truce. Like the U.S. today, the Dutch had nothing to fear from anyone by land or sea; they were more powerful than the rest of the world combined. There was still a state of war with Spain, but the United Provinces were strong and confident enough to grant Madrid a breather. During those twelve years, between 1609 and 1621, instead they decided to quarrel internally.

The times were odd and cruel. A people that had fought for freedom of religion and speech against a foreign ruler were now taking each other to task domestically, and were provoking how-many-angels-fit-on-a-pinhead quarrels. People deliberately bombarded others with fake news pamphlets. Differences of opinion were magnified under a microscope. Under the sham of a church synod, political powerplays were duked out. The end of the story was that the military leader won, the political leader was beheaded, and the political ideologue escaped prison hiding in a book chest.[211]

The Dutch could afford the infighting, because no danger threatened them from outside their borders. After the truce finally expired, Spain was definitively defeated, and the United Provinces was a world power. Not for good, as the country was too small in numbers and area to maintain the status indefinitely, but the achievement was so impressive that it is still taught in schools around the world today.

Equally, the United States can also afford its own equivalent of a Twelve Years' Truce. Its power is unrivaled and unthreatened. The Soviet Union no longer exists, Russia can only stir up trouble regionally and when it does, it does it counterproductively. China is an inherently unstable nation sustained only by keeping its own citizens under its thumb. So far the Chinese approach works, only small groups of people are protesting, and for the time being most of it is peaceful.[212]

Russia has fourteen neighboring countries on its border, including five NATO members, seven if we count the maritime borders with Turkey and Alaska, and only one steadfast military ally, Belarus. China has nineteen neighbors, ten of which claim Chinese territory. Like Russia, it has only one ally, North Korea, and therefore it almost always performs its military exercises by itself. So far, not very effectively - the red team must always win, and twenty percent of practice time is taken up by the mandatory studying of party ideology. It has two aircraft carriers, plus a refurbished flattop that was no longer welcome in the Ukrainian navy. Modern China's military has no war experience. It fought Vietnam briefly in 1979, the hostilities lasted four weeks, and both sides declared victory.

America is bordered by two friendly neighbors and two oceans. It counts 68 military and economic allies, has 572 military bases in 42 countries, and twenty aircraft carriers, not counting the eight that allies England and France have. It has more deep-water surface in the Chesapeake Bay than there is along the entire Asian coast from Russia to India, and, to boot, Maine alone counts so many deepwater harbors that all the world's naval fleets could comfortably anchor there. America has an enviable infrastructure, with 15,000 miles of navigable inland waterways, more than the rest of the world combined. This has significant implications for consumer accessibility. America has been the world's largest consumer market in terms of purchasing power for the past century and a half, now larger than the next five countries combined, China included.[213]

America's lead, in short, over every conceivable competitor can be measured not in meters but in miles, not in years but in decades. And so, in the absence of an enemy outside the gate, Americans are doing what their founders, the Dutch, did four centuries ago. Instead of gazing at the horizon, they stare at their own navel, they bombard each other with fake news, and they magnify the differences between them to the point that consensus and compromise have become curse words.

Silly.

***

Every American has a right to pursue happiness. That's what Thomas Jefferson wrote in the Declaration of Independence, on that imported sheet of paper from Holland.[214] But pursuit is not yet possession: so while waiting for the catch, there can also be unhappiness. In American history, often with reason: slavery, poverty, low wages, women without the right to vote and a lack of other equal treatments, violence in the streets, strikes, integration problems caused by mass immigration, in short, all the obvious and to be expected social sources of unrest. In addition, everyone faces their own private occurrences of unhappiness: every household is confronted with illness at some point, a death in the family, or marital infidelity, addictions, lack of money and other sundry adversity.

Americans who are discontented are often loud about it. At the end of the nineteenth century, it had a population of 75 million. Of these, as many as 30 million had entered the country as immigrants within the previous 30 years. Three-quarters of all New Yorkers were first- or second-generation immigrants. They didn't come to sit on their hands, they came to work. Employment aplenty, it was the golden age of American industrialization. But they often did not yet speak English, they clung to their motherland customs, there was widespread dissatisfaction with their wages, and every so often they went on strike. Moreover, there was still a lot of resentment between North and South. America was more a land of Collected States than truly United States.

Until a war broke out, in 1898. Just a small one; it lasted less than eight months, and Maine had indirectly much to do with it. Spain had sunk the USS Maine, a Navy cruiser, off the coast of Cuba, or at least that's what Joseph Pulitzer's newspaper *New York World* screamed. Pulitzer spent his summers in Bar Harbor, and he came to the defense of the honor of his adopted state, or so he suggested. In reality his paper was competing with New York's other screaming daily, Willam Randolph Hearst's *Journal*, and the louder either paper's headlines, the more copies they sold. It was big news just as dailies began to be read wholesale nationwide.

Pressured by the media, president McKinley declared war on Madrid. Overnight, Americans had a common target to get angry at. Recruiting soldiers to fight in Cuba was easy. Most young men were only too happy to avenge the sunken battleship, even though it would later turn out that the USS Maine had exploded by its crew's own negligence, and that Spain had nothing to do with it.[215] On the corner of Bangor's Ceder and Main Streets, a cruiser's length removed from the Penobscot River, a monument with the ship's bow scrolls today serves as a silent reminder of a key moment in America's, hence the world's, history.

Unity. A foreign enemy. Within two decades, America decided to participate in World War I. That ended what was left of coast-to-coast social discontent. America was henceforth on a general track of unity. With its own contradictions and disagreements, loudly expressed, but by and large a solid majority agreed on the nation's path forward. It came under attack by the Depression, another world war, a witch hunt against alleged communists, civil rights protests and a war in Vietnam, but America has traditionally been a land of blacksmiths. Iron becomes steel if you hammer it hard and long enough.

It lasted for about a hundred years, until 1991. Then, with the implosion of the Soviet Union, the only remaining foreign threat fell away. It caused domestic changes. The level of public discourse plummeted, magnified by the suddenly available megaphone of the internet. In politics, the tool of impeachment was dusted off.[216] It had only been used twice during the first two hundred years of the republic, but was brought back at three more occasions since Washington once again became Nasty Town, each time to no avail other than to enhance the discord.

America elected a Black man as president, twice. Opponents responded with a movement, largely unorganized, an army of malcontents who were not necessarily against an individual but against the unheard-of transformation that the moment embodied. They focused mainly on primaries and tried, successfully, to drive out of office as many moderate politicians as possible. They did so, they claimed, out of love for America, but had a hard time convincing others that, truth told, their principal motive wasn't a strong dislike of other Americans, of those who embraced the upcoming makeover of their country.

Did this happen out of the blue? No, because the same American supremacy that had made the nation a world champion financially, economically and militarily did so also technologically. The United States spearheaded the revolution in the information industry. As we saw earlier, not everyone experiences the age of the internet, automations and robots as an improvement. No one over fifty still lives in the country of their childhood. Everything is changing, much is unknown and uncertain, and even when you call your own bank, you must first press one for English, or else. That's the makeover many have a hard time adapting to.

So there's your discontent, the absence of happiness. Those who were looking for an enemy found one at home, in their laptop, in their smartphone. Multiple others on social media telling them they're right. And they had all the evidence, for look, America is secretly ruled by pedophiles, Jews, and child pornography distributors. Fake news, but so what. Today's America. Where lies trump facts, and where you start warring with your neighbors. All a reality.

And yet all that nastiness, all the moaning, all the carping is destined to go nowhere. Because the good news far outweighs it all.

***

A hand axe in the fist of a Neanderthal was the same size as today's computer mouse. Not only is the difference in application immense, but so is the production history. The hand axe was made spontaneously by one man, from a rock. The mouse is the result of labor and brainwork of thousands, if not more. The internet, the computer, the mouse: all a result of many years in which a large number of people one by one contributed something until your computer mouse here, now, in your hand, under your index finger, does exactly what you want it to do.

Each of us knows this. For everything we have and do, we all depend on others, on each other. And the more each of us blazes their own individualistic trail, the clearer we realize that this is only possible because someone else baked our bread, somebody else somewhere tapped into the oil from which the plastic of our keyboard is made, paved the street, taught our children, and picked the coffee beans that Starbucks turns into ten million cups of coffee every day. That is why Thomas Jefferson's Declaration of Independence was at the same time also very much a Declaration of Interdependence. For the pursuit of happiness and contentment, we depend on a great many others.

Of the 330 million Americans, 170 million are under forty. All born after 1980, raised with computers, the internet, smartphones, and with an access to information like no other generation before them. They have fewer children than before, although in the post-pandemic era demand for fertility services[217] and birth rates have been ticking up again, for the first time since seven years, mainly due to a sharp increase of the number of women working from home.[218] To the degree that the uptick will yet fall short of filling future job openings, immigration will fill the demand sooner or later, as we noticed above. The working population among the next American generation is estimated to increase by ten percent - a crucial contrast with countries like China, Japan and Russia.

They are not a generation of unhappy, malcontented people. Not that they think it's all fun and games, it's not. They take to the streets as soon as once again someone loses their life during a police arrest because of their skin color. They are dead serious about the environment, and they are the big drivers of plant-based food consumption, earning them labels like *climavores* and *climatarians.* They are more likely to drive electric vehicles than older people. This was grounds for car rental company Hertz, immediately after narrowly avoiding bankruptcy in 2021, to order a hundred thousand Tesla's as well as a hundred and seventy-five thousand EV's from General Motors, because Americans aged forty and under constitute by far the largest segment of their customers.[219] As a group, they're purchasing 17 million cars a year. Half of those will be electric by the end of this decade.

Do these members of the younger guard know what they're talking about? You bet they do. They may be bombarded by fake news, but at the same time they were not born yesterday, in particular the women. Universities and colleges attract more women than men; six out of ten graduates are female. They have come to occupy leadership positions left and right, in the media, the automobile industry, tech companies, as police chiefs, as mayors of Portland, Bangor, Boston, San Francisco, Chicago, Seattle, Atlanta, Washington and Las Vegas, and New York City's fire chief: also a woman. For the White House, it is only a matter of time - even Edith, president Wilson's second wife, clandestinely made a first successful attempt already a hundred years ago.

These are not the disaffected who, in the absence of a foreign enemy, want to wage war domestically. These are not a bunch of radicals. They are Americans who realize all too well that they are interdependent. If their employer, or a major manufacturer, does something that they collectively find socially unacceptable, they start a boycott campaign, typically with remarkably quick results. They rely not on the government, not on church, but on family, friends and co-workers. They increasingly work from home, and are inclined to keep doing that. From the comfort of their home, indications are that they work longer hours than economists had predicted, for their work is important to them.[220] They want to be able to rely on their employer.

Only one percent of them still work in agriculture, 24 percent work in factories and make things. Like the Tesla, the mouse, or a more comfortable office chair for the home worker. The other 75 percent provide services, work in medical care, design websites, check customers out at the cash register, serve at Olive Garden or Chipotle, patrol in a police car, put out a fire, or volunteer to serve in the world's most powerful military ever raised.

They are not erecting a gallows in front of the U.S. Capitol. They are not looking for a strongman; quite the opposite. They are the generation of together. They are going to experience setbacks and encounter unexpected problems of sometimes giant proportions, and they are going to bicker, often. But they are also going to amaze the rest of the world, with their captain band of freedom and optimism on their rolled-up sleeve.

Chapter 25

Breaking into the jungle, breaking out of jail

Optimism behind bars

Humanity has been optimistic for ten thousand years, not despite a suspicion that the world may be going to hell, but to the contrary based on a confidence that such an ending is entirely avoidable. Optimism does not depend on geography, on social status or on which generation you happen to be born into. Rich people are optimistic, but so are poor people. Optimists live in the cold, but also in the tropics.

I landed smack dab on the equator, in Macapá at the mouth of the Amazon. The town has built a soccer field and positioned the center circle exactly on the 0 latitude. Every match is one between north and south. The stadium is called Zerao, Portuguese for big zero, and on the road leading up to it an obelisk rises up with a round opening at the top, the circle zero. Landing there reminded me of a story that's well-known among other aviators who have also once landed in Macapá.

It's about a young pilot who went for an after-dinner walk. On the riverbank he met a Brazilian woman, an encounter so cordial that the next morning he decided he was head over heels about her.

He stayed in town for a week and convinced himself that all his dreams had come true, and that she was now his own Brazilian young goddess. He was smitten, and when she asked if he had any money she could borrow, to help her through college, he didn't hesitate. He flew back home, transferred the amount, and never heard from her again. The pilot had been taken to the cleaners.

Optimism was born together with the invention of the knife, and therefore has all that time been aware of its ambivalence. The knife can help and hurt. Managing the difference requires solid agreements, laws, and those who do not abide bear the consequences. The young Brazilian goddess was not only an optimist, she was also an experienced realist. She laid her head down every night on the center of the globe where the truth, like the soccer ball, could roll one way or the other. Her assessment was that she could pull off her trick, as old as mankind, with impunity. She was proven right.

But who is without sin? For while our helicopter crew was having breakfast in Macapá the day after we had arrived, two policemen approached us. Dressed in all black, with border police insignia on their chests. They had seen us take off the previous afternoon at the airport, they said. Which was correct, we had seen them too, in their Blackhawk with no doors. They had each been buckled in one of those doorways, legs out, feet resting on the skids, holding an RF-15. Sharpshooters.

After our landing that previous day, we had taken off again with 20 gallons of extra fuel in four jerrycans. Macapá was to be our final airport in Brazil, and the distance to the next airport, Cayenne in French Guiana, was too far to cover in one flight. So we decided to build our own little refueling station.

We flew an hour out of Macapá and landed in a clearing in the rainforest. We put the jerrycans on the ground there, covered them with jungle leaves, and I stored the location in the GPS, calling it "22", two times two jerrycans. Then we took off again and returned to Macapá. In all, the helicopter had used two hours of fuel, so we requested a refill and looked forward to the next day with confidence. With the help of our own little gas station at 22, there would be enough fuel to make it all the way to Cayenne.

However, what we did was illegal. At the final airport before an aircraft leaves a country, you go to the immigration office and you check yourself and your aircraft out. It's what we had to do in Chile, in Puerto Montt when for three days in a row we made multiple failed attempts to cross the Andes, and in Brazil it was no different. Once you take off, you are not allowed to land again until after you have crossed the border, where you become the next country's responsibility. A helicopter's fuel tank limitations, that was not Brazil's problem. We were supposed to abide by their law.

That is why they have a border police with Blackhawks and officers in black outfits. They do nothing but trying to find violators of their laws in the rainforest. Those who attempt to evade them and land small planes or helicopters are automatically presumed to be engaged in drugs trafficking. The snipers on board don't first ask.

The two officers looked friendly. One of them asked where we were from, and if those small Robinson-44s were any fun flying. And then, "What's the reach, how far do they fly?" Damn, trick question. What if I told the truth, and they'd do a quick calculation in their heads? On the other hand, they didn't yet know where we were headed today. We could just as easily be planning on making another domestic flight. Maybe we were heading back south, toward Rio where we had narrowly escaped those cable car wires three thousand miles ago, courtesy of a concrete Christ the Redeemer standing two thousand feet above the city with his arms wide handing out blessings. Then it didn't matter what we said.

We cracked both gentlemen our broadest smiles, and replied, "Farther than you'd think." The gentlemen smiled back.

***

Breaking the law sometimes does relate to helicopters, hope, and optimism. This has to do with flying as a symbol of freedom, a phenomenon recognized by many who have once or twice dreamed that they were capable of flying, of floating in the air. But it is especially appreciated by those who lack all semblances of freedom day in and day out, men and women who did indeed break the law and are locked up in prison.

Outside the town of Jessup, Maryland, there are two maximum security correctional facilities, one for each gender. Some of their inmates have done terrible things, others have been repeatedly guilty of drug related offenses. A little-known fact of prison life is that out of every ten inmates, on average only two can properly read and write. The rest are functionally illiterate. That's one reason why they end up on the wrong path, because it can be a big challenge finding and keeping a decent job if you cannot read what is written on signs, boxes and forms. Crime is then more easily accessible, and it usually pays better, too.

In prisons, inmates fantasize about helicopters. Even more so in max-security facilities where they have no prospect of being released for many years to come. For those who are locked up, all doors are hermetically sealed, and even if an aspiring escapee would manage to navigate that barrier, the three lines of walls and fences beyond it are impregnable. Prisons no longer use concertinas of barbed wire. They have been replaced by razor concertina wires which do major damage to skin and flesh if you try to climb them. Prison breaks hardly ever occur anymore, not without outside help. Hence the fantasy about helicopters. Once in a while they do happen. A helicopter then suddenly appears overhead, low, the escapee is pulled on board, and off they go.

It comes with no guarantees of freedom. Some fifty recorded attempts have been made worldwide, and almost always the fugitive was quickly recaptured. Unlike an inconspicuous getaway car, a helicopter stands out like nothing else once it lands to unload the prisoner. Moreover, using a helicopter to free jailbirds is almost always the result of a hijacking - the inmate's accomplice sticks a gun to the pilot's head and forces them to fly to the penitentiary. After the bad guys and the gun have left, the pilot immediately radioes the police. Sometimes he holds down the radio button while still arguing with the hijackers in flight, without them realizing what he is doing. In that case air traffic control listens in, and the police are waiting at the landing spot.

France, the country of Alexandre Dumas and Monte Cristo, his master escapee, is the world champion of helicopter escapes, eleven attempts between 1981 and 2018. Therefore, it is not surprising that the world record holder of prison breaks is also a Frenchman, Pascal Payet, jailed for killing the driver of a cash transport truck. Payet himself escaped twice by helicopter, and a third time he forced one to fly to the same prison, to help a few cellmates escape as well. Each time he was caught, underscoring that while success is not impossible, it is improbable.

This didn't deter Nadine Vaujour. She was the young wife of a bank robber. The day after Michel Vaujour was arrested in Paris, she began taking helicopter flight instruction just outside the city. She paid in cash, and the flight school knew no better than that her name was Lena Rigot. Nadine, who in her spare time was also raising their two daughters, passed her solo test, and on May 26, 1986, she flew low over Paris to the heavily guarded Prison De La Sainté. Traffic controllers watched her on radar, and summoned her to stay away from downtown, but Nadine ignored them. She came to a hover above the prison roof, the only unguarded part of the facility, lowered a rope and Michel climbed aboard. Nadine then flew to a soccer field, where they abandoned the helicopter.[221]

End of story? No. Three months later, they were both arrested as they were about to open their own café in Paris. Michel resisted and took a bullet to the head; Nadine surrendered. She went behind bars for a few years, and Michel was locked up for seventeen years, spending most of that time in solitary confinement. After his release and miraculous recovery, he wrote a book, *Love Saved Me From Sinking*. However, that did not refer to Nadine who had risked everything to keep her amour outside the prison walls. Michel divorced her while incarcerated, and remarried his lawyer.[222]

***

In Jessup, I went to prison. I did it together with Alice who, during my expedition, had also started taking flying lessons. She passed her tests and obtained her license. She learned during her instruction that there are very few female pilots who can fly both helicopters and airplanes, only two hundred and fifty in the U.S., and this inspired her to get that fixed-wing license as well: two hundred and fifty-one.

Together we flew to a small airport near Jessup, and we reported to the entrance of the women's prison. We were expected, the warden was happy to have us come talk to a room full of inmates. The inside of an American prison looks pretty much like what most people have seen in TV drama series, overcrowded, chaotic, loud, and the absolute opposite of a luxury hotel that outsiders sometimes paint. Large dormitories with bunk beds, everyone wearing the same drab shirts and pants, and a total lack of privacy. In maximum security facilities, there are no TV sets and soda machines in break rooms with easy chairs. Each day is exactly like yesterday and all the tomorrows will be too, as drab as the garb they wear.

Matthew of Galilee, the tax collector who quit his job for the sake of an uncertain existence as a roadie for a superstar from Nazareth, was the guy of "do not worry about tomorrow." But he talked about more than just that. He also mentioned feeding the hungry, giving the thirsty something to drink, and clothing the naked. And he added: visit a prisoner now and then.[223] So we did that. We came to talk to them about hope when all seems hopeless. We came joking about helicopters and saying that we couldn't understand why we didn't get permission to land in the exercise yard. Watching the women laugh. Helping them to enjoy one hour to be different from all the other drab hours inside the four walls.

During such prison visits Alice would tell them that at some future point opportunities will open outside prison. That she herself, a plumber's daughter, never thought she would one day rise above the trees and the rooftops. Big eyes in the room. The pin you can hear drop. And then, at the end, the exchanging of quick hugs. What is not allowed in the visitors' hall, touching, is allowed when we come to talk about aspiring to a new horizon. Hugging, encouraging, listening as they say they miss their children. That they hope their own daughters will make different choices.

What are you in here for, I ask Jane whose name I write in the book I sign for her as a gift, even though chances are she may never be able to read it. Drugs, she replies, assault. With a gun?

No, she says. A knife.

* * *

"Farther than you'd think." The border policemen in Macapá were satisfied with our response and went along with Sigurveig shooting a group photo. We quickly made our way out, off to the airport where we checked out and got our passports stamped, and an hour later we were on the ground in the jungle, at "22". The two times two jerrycans were waiting for us under the leaves, and although traffic control in Macapá could see on the radar that we had stopped somewhere in the rain-forest, no Blackhawk appeared. We refueled, took off again, and after two hours we landed without incident in French Guiana. There, automobiles have French license plates, payment is in euros, and you quickly understand why it used to be one big French prison.

This is the place where France, for centuries notorious for its barbaric prison practices, used to bring its longest-sentenced prisoners. Forbiddingly hot, desolate and far away from home. Anyone who came here was expected to die here. They'd chain them together in pairs and sit them on wooden boats in Cayenne's harbor, on bread and water, in the tropical heat, until the wood rotted away under their feet and they'd drown, to-gether. The least survivable place was an island off the coast, Devil's Island. The French government once sent fifteen pros-titutes there, in a sudden rehabilitation attempt. It was hoped that the women would persuade the tough guys to lead regular lives and start families. No children were born. But just about the entire island population did contract syphilis.[224]

Yet even under all these hopeless circumstances, some did not abandon hope. Sometimes an escape attempt succeeded and then the news would reach the French mainland, usually along with the fugitive prisoner himself who typically was once again arrested. But once in a while it worked out, and so in France a tradition of spectacular escapes was born. For what went wrong last time may next time be avoidable. Thus hope triumphs over experience, behind bars like everywhere else.

Chapter 26

Epilogue: When it actually does hit the fan

In the summer of 2007 the helicopter covered a distance of 40,000 miles. It translated to 97 days, 316 flight hours, 175 landings, 30 days on the ground, 67 days in the air, 5,000 gallons of fuel, including gasoline that we fetched 12 times from roadside gas stations in 8 countries, and 5 refuels from barrels we had suppliers pre-deliver to airstrips in Canada and Alaska, 20 countries, 29 border crossings, and overnight stays in 73 different hotel beds. Two records: we were the first to fly the distance from Barrow in Alaska to Ushuaia in Argentina by helicopter, and also the first to circle the entire South American continent. To the best of my knowledge, the records have not been broken since, and the best of knowledge is all I can go by since Guinness World Records does not keep track of most aviation records.

Risky? You are what you risk, said economist Michelle Wucker about Annie Edson, the first human to successfully drop down the Niagara Falls. I decided that a super-long helicopter flight was in essence no more risky than spending an hour in an automobile on the ground. Every day there are 1.2 billion cars on roadways worldwide.[225] No one hesitates to join the race. My estimate was shockingly realistic. With only few exceptions, the taxi rides to and from airports were invariably the riskiest stretches, especially in countries like Mexico, Peru and Guyana.

There were tense moments. Crossing the Darien Gap between Panama and Colombia was risky because the nature of the terrain made emergency landings virtually impossible. Colombia itself was at the time a high-risk area, with guerrilla fighters and warring drug cartels on the ground in dense jungles. The control tower at the airport of Cali recommended a cruising altitude of five thousand feet above what in the southwestern part of the country was known as Murder Alley, because that would keep us out of bullet striking range, they said. But that day the cloud ceiling refused to lift any higher than four thousand feet, which kept our blood pressure elevated until we safely made it to neighboring Ecuador.

When we came back to Colombia seven weeks later, now coming up from the southeast, we landed in Montería, ground zero of what was then popularly described as Kidnap Alley. Our intention was to refuel and then quickly make our way to safe Panama City, but there was a storm system hanging around the border, and so we were left with no choice but to spend the night in Montería. Beside us on the airfield apron a small plane was parked with no identifying markings. The pilot was flying for Brinks, the valuables transportation company. Their armored trucks did not drive across the country, he told me. Money was flown, airlifted without registering a flight plan. In Montería that evening, night and the next early morning, no one ventured into the streets. Downtown seemed deserted.

But none of this came as a surprise; these were not facts that shocked, much less overwhelmed us. In the risk assessment that was made beforehand, we knew these were the bottlenecks, the potential trouble spots. It's not something you worry about because, while the day will come that they need to be confronted, it's not now, it's the day of tomorrow or beyond. It puts no dent in optimism. Every day, people moved from one place to the next through these very same areas, and ninety-nine times out of a hundred, they encountered no problem. The only difference with us was that we were flying relatively low over insurgent territory in a white helicopter, a means of transportation that guerrillas and cocaine manufacturers on the ground would probably consider belonging to the police.

We thought about it, knowing that security guarantees do not exist in life, and decided that the summons of challenge weighed heavier than its uncertainty. The final decision about committing ourselves to an expedition like this rested with the owner of the helicopter, and that was me. I felt no hesitation. At some point all you have is a solid belief, a confidence that it's going to be fine, that it's going to work out. Not knowing for sure, yet feeling good about it, that's optimism.

***

Remember the metaphor of those quaking aspens at the beginning of this book? The theory that suggests that all events inevitably flow from one another, like a colony of aspen trees that all emerge from the same root system, from the same one tree seed. President Woodrow Wilson's wife died, world war one was raging, he barely grieved because he fell into the arms of a young widow who anointed him God's servant on Earth, and before everyone realized what was happening, it led to world war two. An inevitable chain of events. Or is it?

Let's see.

In the morning of July 20, 2009, thunder rumbled in South Carolina. I was by then living there with Alice in a house on a landing strip. The United States counts more than six hundred airparks, communities of pilots who own a private aircraft and share a runway together. It's a pleasant way of living, with neighbors who all have the same hobby. Long-time Maine resident John Travolta lives in such an airpark. In ours, we were the only ones with a helicopter.

I needed to visit my office in Maryland that day. We had a choice to make: nine hours by car or four hours by helicopter. If we wanted to fly, we had to hurry, because the thunderstorm was coming. We decided on the rush. In a house on an airstrip, you don't have a garage, you have a hangar. We pushed the helicopter out, loaded Chopper the dog in the back, and took off, just ahead of the squall that was approaching. Four hours later, we were in Maryland. It was two years to the day since we had narrowly escaped the sixteen cables between Sugarloaf Mountain's two peaks in Rio de Janeiro.

While in Maryland, I received a phone call from the flight school, the place where a few years earlier I had overheard pilots vowing they would "absolutely not" ever make my superlong-distance flight. The owner was the father of a special-needs son, and together he and I had started a foundation that was raising funds for at-risk youth like his boy, money that would go to professional help and guidance. We had named it Helicopter Explorers for Life Partnerships, HELP for short. He asked if they could borrow my helicopter.

The foundation had organized an event at another airport across the Catoctin hills. People could buy tickets for a 10-minute sightseeing flight, with the proceeds going to the charity. The helicopter they normally used for such events had a few days earlier made a hard landing somewhere and was out of commission. I said yes, of course. There'd be two pilots on board, both themselves flight instructors, both professionals.

At the end of the afternoon of sightseeing and charity flying, bad weather hit the area. The pilots and a foundation delegation stayed on the ground and waited for the storm to blow over. They called the flight school to let them know, and someone there offered to drive over and come get them by car. They could leave the helicopter at the other airport and pick her up the next day. But they said they'd wait it out and declined the offer.

At a quarter past ten in the evening, they took their chances. They lifted off, ran into low-hanging clouds near the hills, descended, flew low and slow over an interstate highway to get their bearings, and then hit an overhead power line. The helicopter crashed, caught fire and was completely destroyed. All four on board were killed.[226]

***

This was the helicopter that was, in fact, the real record setter, that had done all the heavy lifting and had held her own in all the conditions that we had unleashed on her. Now, twenty miles from base, what we had narrowly avoided two years and seventeen thousand miles earlier happened to this helicopter after all. Newspapers began calling, radio, television, journalists came knocking on the front door. In the first twenty-four hours alone, according to Google, more than twelve hundred news stories about the crash appeared worldwide, each attracted by the magnet of bad news.

Every day... All land safely... Not a word about it... Until one drops out of the sky...

Quaking aspen: what if in South Carolina we had decided to take the car and just leave the helicopter in the hangar? Then I wouldn't have been able to donate her for a few hours in Maryland, and the four dead would still be alive. Then four families would not be grieving, and the lives of all those children that

I watched saying goodbye to two fathers and a mother at four funerals would have taken a totally different course.

Was all this the inevitable, inescapable, unavoidable consequence of one decision? No, because I could have refused to let them use my helicopter for charity. Or the pilot could have accepted the offer to have himself and the three others be picked up. He could have decided not to take off that night, period. He could have turned around immediately upon spotting the clouds in the hills. He could have simply parked the helicopter on the Interstate as soon as he had made eye contact with it, and taken the inconvenience to traffic for what it was. Nothing was inevitable, everything was avoidable.

But shit happens, it did occur, the National Transportation Safety Board did a thorough investigation and concluded after a year: pilot error.[227] It reported its findings which were distributed among all pilots around the world. Somewhere, who knows, this prevented a similar accident, maybe because one or two, or ten, pilots decided not to take off after all, because the weather, the sky, the clouds don't look good. Because, remember reading about that crash in Maryland? That guy was offered a free ride so he might as well sleep at home, and if only he had.

The flight from South Carolina, that morning with the dog in the back seat, ahead of the thunderstorm, was my last. I haven't been in a helicopter since that day again. At first because the aftermath of an aviation accident keeps an aircraft owner in the crosshairs of dueling insurance companies and their lawyers for years. But once that dust had settled, what rested was this simple assessment: what had been achieved, I wasn't going to top. My aviation challenge was over. No use trying to replicate what was already successfully done and completed. And that's how the helicopter's spare keys now hang from the arm of crucifix-Jesus on the wall across from my desk. For good. The original keys were lost in the crash.

Sometimes a moment arrives when you feel and know, don't push it, don't fly closer to the sun, this is my limit. Gotta leave the next move to others. And that's realism.

Then again, what was it that the dictionary guy said, John Simpson? "You should never give up." Who knows, perhaps.
The future is still young.

*****

Chapter 27

Notes and Sources

1. ^ Stephen King, *On Writing, A Memoir of the Craft*, p41.
2. ^ After all was said and done, one out of every six newspaper copies in the U.S. would be printed on paper made by Garrett Schenck's company.
3. ^ http://www.rehabchicago.org/the-human-brain/
4. ^ Psalm 103:8. For the weeds part, see the chapter about the single men and women of Russia and China for a detailed breakdown.
5. ^ CBC radio, *The inventor of the Rubik's Cube took this long to first solve it*, March 13, 2021.
6. ^ David Kind, *How Lego patents helped build a toy empire, brick by brick*, Smithsonian Magazine, Feb. 7, 2019, also: Mauro Guillén, *2030, How Today's Biggest Trends Will Collide and Reshape the Future of Everything*, p228.
7. ^ Herman Melville, the author of *Moby Dick*, mentioned in his book as early as 1851 what was apparently a prototype of the Swiss army pocket knife. Melville had visited Switzerland ten years earlier.
8. ^ It was not my first shot at setting a record. In 2004, I had organized a mass book-signing event at a shopping mall for published authors. A record 153 authors

participated, and it earned us a certificate from Guinness World Records. Sam Yu, *Authors have write stuff for record*, Frederick News Post, March 1, 2004.

9. ^ Barrow today officially has a different name, Utqiagvik. The headland outside the village is still called Point Barrow.

10. ^ Barbara Morgan, *Wilson, Edith Bolling (1872–1961)*, Encyclopedia.com.

11. ^ Jan Willem Schulte Nordholt, *Woodrow Wilson, A Life for World Peace*, p59.

12. ^ Historian-lawyer James Robenalt describes a multitude of reaction occurrences such as those surrounding the death of Woodrow Wilson's first wife and the consequences thereafter for two world wars in *January 1973, Watergate, Roe vs. Wade, Vietnam and the Month That Changed America Forever*.

13. ^ Unilever hired Zamora's services and made commercials using his work, for one of the company's skin care products. They have since been viewed tens of millions of times on YouTube.

14. ^ Melanie Tannenbaum, *Optimism in Seniors Predicts Fewer Chronic Illnesses, Better Overall Health*, Scientific American, Sept. 29, 2015, also: Galadriel Watson, *Why some people are more optimistic than others - and why it matters*, Washington Post, Aug. 17, 2020.

15. ^ Robert Plomin, Michael Scheier, C.S. Bergeman, N.L. Pedersen, J.R. Nesselroade and G.E McClearn, *Optimism, pessimism and mental health: A twin/adoption analysis*, ScienceDirect: Personality and Individual Differences, Volume 13, Issue 8, August 1992, pp921-930.

16. ^ Daniel Kahneman, *Thinking Fast and Slow*, p256.

17. ^ My crew mates and fellow adventurers were photographer Sigurveig Palmadottir and pilot Stephan Goldberg.

My own primary cockpit responsibility was that of being the flight navigator.

18. ^ Bay City Times Press, Oct 12, 1901.

19. ^ The Boston Globe, undated, last week of Oct. 1901.

20. ^ Michelle Wucker, *You Are What You Risk*, pp1-4.

21. ^ It happened on Oct. 5, 2020, at a store of the Hannaford supermarket chain in Saco, Maine. The perpetrator had been fired from a pizza manufacturer that supplied prepackaged dough to the supermarket. Video footage showed him opening a package in a refrigerated section, putting something in it, and leaving the store without purchasing anything. The dough was sold, the blade was discovered by the customer, nobody got hurt, but Hannaford suffered a quarter million dollar loss from returned packs of pizza dough. The perp pleaded guilty and received a five-year prison sentence. Neil Vigdor, *Man Who Planted Razor Blades in Pizza Dough Gets 5 Years in Prison*, New York Times, Dec. 2, 2021.

22. ^ United States Centers for Disease Control and Prevention report, Jan 19, 2018.

23. ^ John Simpson, *The Word Detective*, p192.

24. ^ Jonathan Gottschall, *The Storytelling Animal, How Stories Make Us Human*, p42.

25. ^ Ibid, p34. Gottschall quotes from a study of 360 stories that playing children told each other. They were about mothers and babies, monsters and heroes, spaceships and unicorns, but the common denominator each time was: danger, trouble.

26. ^ Ibid.

27. ^ Gottschall, p27.

28. ^ Data from Central Bureau of Statistics, the Netherlands.

29. ^ Patricia Cohen: *Next big thing: knowing they know that you know*, New York Times, March 31, 2010.

30. ^ Max Roser, *Humans destroyed forests for thousands of years - we can become the first generation that achieves a world in which forests expand*, Our World in Data, Oxford University, April 20, 2022.

31. ^ Specifically, demographers on behalf of the nonprofit Population Reference Bureau in Washington, DC and of the United Nations.

32. ^ Toshiko Kaneda and Carl Haub, *How Many People Have Ever Lived on Earth*, Population Reference Bureau, May 18, 2021.

33. ^ There is one researcher who suspects, based on a skeleton find in Morocco, that we could be three hundred thousand years old, but for the total number of people on Earth, this wouldn't make much difference. In those extra hundred thousand years, the species would have been close to extinction on several occasions due to far too low birth rates. Ewen Callaway, *Oldest Homo sapiens fossil claim rewrites our species' history*, Nature, June 7, 2017.

34. ^ Oliver Burkeman, *Four Thousand Weeks, Time Management for Mortals*, loc. 57.

35. ^ Bee Wilson, *Consider the Fork, A History of How We Cook*, loc. 285.

36. ^ Ibid, loc 290.

37. ^ *Excavations reveal daily life of 10,000 years ago*, Hürriyet, Sept. 20, 2012.

38. ^ Michael Shellenberger, *Apocalypse Never, Why Environmental Alarmism Hurts Us All*, p133, also: *Fire and the Brain, How Cooking Shaped Humans*, American Museum of National History.

39. ^ Linda Jaivin, *Origins*, p10.

40. ^ Wilson, p43.

41. ^ The only function of the fork until then was to pin food to the plate while it was being cut. The wife of doge

Domenico Selvo of Venice used a fork to lift food to her mouth, to the horror of Cardinal Petrus Damiani of Ostia, who wrote about it a thousand years ago. He envisioned that her body "entirely rotted away." Margaret Visser, *Rituals of Dinner, The Origins, Evolution, Eccentricities, and Meaning of Table Manners*, p189.

42. ^ Ibid, p186.

43. ^ The gunman was 19-year-old Gavrilo Prinzip. Because of his age he escaped the death penalty. He died in prison before the end of the war, probably of tuberculosis. More about him in the chapter about the 20th century being the worst and the best.

44. ^ Thomas Fleming, *Napoleon's Invasion of North America*, in: *The Collected What If, Eminent Historians Imagine What Might Have Been*, pp534-551.

45. ^ Jules Witcover, *Lincoln's Successor Problem*, Politico Magazine, Apr 13, 2015, also: Chicago Tribune, Nov. 16, 2014.

46. ^ Having become US president upon Lincoln's death in 1865, Andrew Johnson appointed Hamlin Collector of the Port of Boston, a lucrative federal position. Hamlin resigned within a year, in protest.

47. ^ Larry Zuckerman, *Potato, How the Humble Spud Rescued the Western World*, p192. The exact number of deaths in Ireland due to the famine has never been established. One million dead in Ireland itself is a widely accepted figure, but more than a million Irish also hurried to leave as soon as the famine broke out. Among them were an unknown and uncounted number of additional casualties. Before the potato blight of 1845, 8 million people lived in Ireland. In the six decades following the Great Famine, 5 million Irish emigrated. By the time World War I broke out, Ireland's population was only half of what it was in the mid-nineteenth century.

48. ^ William Bernstein, *Masters of the Word, How Media Shaped History from the Alphabet to the Internet*, p14.

49. ^ In my biography of Warren Harding, *De verliefde president* (Balans, Amsterdam 2021), I describe in detail how popular Harding in 1916 already was as a senator. He was a journalist by trade, the publisher and editor-in-chief of a regional daily in Ohio, who, in return for publishing railroad companies' departure and arrival schedules, had 5,000 free railroad miles available, every year. Across America, voters knew him. In 1916, with Harding absent from the ticket, Wilson won narrowly, after taking the state of Ohio by a few votes. When Harding eventually did run for president in 1920, his opposing candidate was also from Ohio. Nevertheless, Harding beat him by half a million more Ohio votes. He would in 1916 almost certainly have beaten Wilson in his home state that year. In that case, he, not Woodrow Wilson, would have determined what the Treaty of Versailles would have looked like in 1919.

50. ^ The budgeted construction cost of the Maginot Line was 3 billion French francs. The real expense got completely out of hand and roughly doubled. The dollar amount reflects today's currency value.

51. ^ In 1879, Swedish explorer Adolf Erik Nordenskiöld managed to sail along the entire Euro-Asian coastline and reach the Bering Strait between Siberia and Alaska, but not until after his ship had spent the entire winter ice-locked.

52. ^ Tim Harford, *The Data Detective*, p21.

53. ^ Han van Meegeren was in fact an admirer of the Nazis. In 1942, a book about his art, *Teekeningen 1*, was published, and after the war a copy was found in the ruins of Adolf Hitler's chancellery, signed in German by Van Meegeren: *"Den geliebten Führer in dankbarer Anerkennung gewidmet*

von H. van Meegeren, Laren, North Holland 1942." Translation: "Dedicated with gratitude to the beloved Führer." Het Parool, June 17, 1945.

54. ^ But not in Hollywood. The film *The Last Vermeer* premiered in 2019, about Van Meegeren's deception that Abraham Bredius fell for. It was released during the Covid epidemic and after a few weeks the movie was temporarily taken out of circulation. Since then it has had a successful second life via television and the Internet.

55. ^ Harford, p33.

56. ^ David Rooney, *About Time, A History of Civilization in Twelve Clocks*, p11.

57. ^ William Bernstein, *Birth of Plenty, How the Prosperity of the Modern World Was Created*, pp3 and 385.

58. ^ The oldest example goes back to 3,500 years ago when someone in Mesopotamia wrote the origin story of the local Gilgamesh mythology on a clay tablet.

59. ^ Howard Reid and Justin Pollard, *Rise and Fall of Alexandria*, p89.

60. ^ Nate Silver, *The Signal and the Noise*, p2.

61. ^ Tom Standage, *The Victorian Internet*, pp2, 23 and 27.

62. ^ Standage, pp8-9.

63. ^ Standage, p40.

64. ^ Claude Chappe is buried at the Père Lachaise cemetery in Paris. On his tomb sits a miniature version of his semaphore.

65. ^ Eric Gastfriend, *90% of all the Scientists who Ever Lived are Alive Today*, www.ericgastfriend.com.

66. ^ *Maine Population and Demographics*, https://namecensus.com/demographics/maine/.

67. ^ Steven Pinker, *The Better Angels of Our Nature, Why Violence Has Declined*, p28.

68. ^ John Koehler, *Stasi*, pp141-148.

69. ^ Ammon Shea, *The Phone Book, The Curious History of the Book That Everyone Uses But No One Reads*, p7.

70. ^ Ibid, p16.

71. ^ Brad Stone, *The Everything Store: Jeff Bezos And The Age Of Amazon*, Chapter 2. Stone quotes Jeff Bezos saying in 1994, talking about the Amazon, "This is not only the largest river in the world, it's many times larger than the next big river. It blows all other rivers away." That's true in terms of the total amount of water that flows through it. The Amazon carries more water than the next seven largest rivers combined.

72. ^ The domain name still exists. Click on it, and you'll land on Amazon's website.

73. ^ There are exceptions to the rule. The Vietnam Helicopter Pilots Association (VHPA) estimates that during the Vietnam War between 1961 and 1975, more than one hundred thousand pilots and crew members served. Their chance of crashing was 1 in 20: more than 4,800 of them died in military action. Source: Arlington Military Cemetery.

74. ^ Jennifer Lee, *The Fortune Cookies Chronicles*, p3.

75. ^ Ibid, p13. It took a judge in 1983 to determine where fortune cookies were first invented, in San Francisco or in Los Angeles. Both sides proved that cookies did exist in their cities before World War I. The judge went for San Francisco, and thereby anointed the original inventor - who was not Chinese, but Japanese.

76. ^ Patrick Wyman, *The Verge, Reformation, Renaissance, and Forty Years That Shook the World, 1490-1530*, p60. Wyman draws on what Diego de Valera wrote in *Memorial de diversas hazañas*, pp47-48.

77. ^ Her real name was *Gruoch ingen Boite* and she married Macbeth, after he had killed her first husband. Macbeth became king of Scotland, Gruoch became queen, and her

son from her first marriage eventually succeeded Macbeth. The queen had a reputation for getting whatever she set her mind to, at any price.

78. ^ Marilyn Yalom, *Birth of the Chess Queen*, p68.

79. ^ Willem Meiners, *Greenland Isn't Green, And There's No Danish in Denmark*, p127.

80. ^ The joy was relatively short-lived. After a volcanic eruption in Iceland hampered international air traffic across 20 countries for a week in 2010, and was still paralyzing some flight routes three more months later, Icelandair decided on a reputation fix. From then on, it named its planes after volcanoes.

81. ^ Arthur Herman, *The Viking Heart, How Scandinavians Conquered the World*, p101.

82. ^ Vigdis Finnbogadottir was president of Iceland from 1980 to 1996. To date, no other elected woman has served any country as head of state for that length of time.

83. ^ One-third of the world's lava flows from Icelandic volcanoes.

84. ^ Jess Distil, *Ask An...Elf Expert: Do Elves Disrupt Construction Work?* Reykjavik Grapevine, 9 Oct 2020, also: Svala Ragnar, *Elven safety: the rocky homes of Iceland's 'hidden people,'* The Guardian, March 25, 2015.

85. ^ The high suicide rate in the U.S. is a direct result of its widespread and legally protected gun ownership. More than half of successful suicide attempts involve the use of a firearm. Nonetheless, gun owners are not more suicidal than others. The difference is in the effectiveness of a gunshot as the chosen method: 85 percent effective. Many more suicide attempts in America are made by using drug overdoses, but these are only effective in three percent of all cases. Madelin Drexler, *Guns & Suicide, The Hidden Toll*, Harvard Public Health magazine.

86. ^ Fuschia Sirois, *Why optimists live longer than the rest of us*, Washington Post, July 3, 2022, also: Victoria Masterson, *Women are more likely to live past 90 if they're optimistic, according to a new study*, World Economic Forum, June 29, 2022.

87. ^ D.A. Snowdon, S.J. Kemper, J.A. Mortimer, L.H. Greiner, D.R. Wegsein and W.R. Markesbery, *Linguistic ability in early life and cognitive function and Alzheimer's disease in late life. Findings from the Nun Study*, National Library of Medicine, Feb 21, 1996.

88. ^ James Ward, *The Perfection of the Paper Clip*, p3.

89. ^ Olivia Waxman, *The 5 Most Surprising Inventions to Come Out of World War I*, Time Magazine, 6 april 2017.

90. ^ Jake Swearingen, *An Idea That Stuck: How George de Mestral Invented the Velcro Fastener*, New York Magazine, 24 november 2016.

91. ^ Dava Sobel, *Longitude, The True Story of a Lone Genius Who Solved the Greatest Scientific Problem of His Time*, p15.

92. ^ Alexander Lee, *The Ugly Renaissance, Sex, Greed, Violence and Depravity in an Age of Beauty*, p11.

93. ^ Greg Steinmetz, *The Richest Man Who Ever Lived*, p70. For instance, Fugger provided one of the powerful men he financed with bodyguards, a team of mercenaries from Switzerland. The Swiss Guard still guards the pope today. It earned Fugger the nickname God's Banker. He made himself all but indispensable to the powerful because he kept bank branches throughout Europe. This allowed clients to withdraw large sums of money without first having to transport it on horseback across half the continent. Fugger thus put an end to the robbery of large cash transports over land.

94. ^ Wyman, p12.

95. ^ Bernstein, p18.

96. ^ A.J. Wright, *Astonishing Numbers: Vaccine Efforts In the 1918 Flu Pandemic*, Clinical Oncology News, July 8, 2020.

97. ^ Data provided by Statista in Hamburg and the World Bank.

98. ^ DeNeen L. Brown, *Lynchings in Mississippi never stopped*, Washington Post, Aug. 8, 2021.

99. ^ Pinker, p191, also: Nassim Nicholas Taleb, *The Black Swan*, p40. Bertrand Russell was originally talking about a chicken instead of a turkey, but with a similar connotation.

100. ^ Hannah Ritchie and Max Roser, *Plastic Pollution*, Our World in Data, Oxford University, April 2022.

101. ^ Hannah Ritchie: *Ocean plastics: How much do rich countries contribute by shipping their waste overseas?* Our World in Data, Oxford University, Oct 11, 2022.

102. ^ Mathew White, Jr, *The Great Big Book of Horrible Things, The Definitive Chronicle of History's 100 Worst Atrocities.*

103. ^ Pinker, p208.

104. ^ Liaquat Ahamed, *Lords of Finance, The bankers who broke the world*, p21.

105. ^ Hjalmar Schacht, *The Stabilization of the Mark*, p105. There were 133 printing plants operating day and night in Germany, with 1783 presses continuously printing banknotes.

106. ^ Guus Pikkemaat, *Eleanore of Aquitaine, an extraordinary woman in the summer tide of the Middle Ages*, p283. Pikkemaat was impressed by Eleanore his entire life, putting into practice what he learned from her. He became a newspaper editor in 1963 and immediately began hiring women journalists. Year after year, his Dutch newspaper received an award for who employed the most female reporters.

107. ^ Today the state of Maine operates the Dorothea Dix Psychiatric Center in Bangor, providing excellent care for Maine's severest mentally ill patients.

108. ^ David Halberstam, *The Best and the Brightest*, p268.

109. ^ Paul Hendrickson, *McNamara, Specters of Vietnam*, Washington Post, May 10, 1984.

110. ^ Ernest May and Philip Zelikow, *The Kennedy Tapes: Inside the White House during the Cuban Missile Crisis*, p33.

111. ^ *The Kennedy's: Dear Ros*, Time Magazine, Feb. 23, 1970.

112. ^ New York Times, March 17, 1996.

113. ^ The meeting of delegations from the U.S., Cuba and the Soviet Union took place in Moscow Jan. 27-28, 1989, more than 26 years after the missile crisis.

114. ^ Pinker, p208.

115. ^ Frank Sedlar, *The Trussed Concrete Steel Company and Albert Kahn*, Engineering Industrial Architecture, Apr 23, 2013.

116. ^ Today's value, in 1968 it was $170 billion.

117. ^ Antoinella Lazeri, *If I hadn't spotted that the sea was fizzing then my parents, sister and me would all be dead*, The Sun, Dec 26, 2014.

118. ^ Data American Cancer Society, Jan 12, 2022.

119. ^ The Daily Mirror, Jan 22, 1992, also: Tampa Bay Times, Jan 22, 1992.

120. ^ Jessica Hornig, *From Fear to Survival: Knowledge Is Key*, ABC 20/20, Jan 20, 2009.

121. ^ The year was 1540. His actual date of birth that year is unknown.

122. ^ Elsevier and its British merger partner Reed are now together listed as RELX. Ranked second and third on the list of largest publishers are Thomson Reuters and Bertelsmann. Jim Milliot, Publishers Weekly, Sept. 21, 2021.

123. ^ Andrew Pettegree and Arthur der Weduwen, *The Book-shop of the World, Making and Trading Books in the Dutch Golden Age*, p1.

124. ^ In addition, unique in the world, Amsterdam at the time also counted six competing newspapers. Ibid. p68.

125. ^ *Explosion Aboard TWA Flight 800; Storm Delay Saves a Life*, New York Times, July 19, 1996.

126. ^ Steven Jay Russell, *Jim Carrey Made A Movie About Me. Here's What It Didn't Show About Life In Prison*, Huffington Post, Sept. 4, 2018.

127. ^ *I Love You Philip Morris* ran in theaters for four months and became available on DVD in 2011.

128. ^ William Bernstein, *Masters of the Word, How Media Shaped History from the Alphabet to the Internet*, p9.

129. ^ Dominic Lane, *The leap that defined a life: Hans Conrad Schumann*, Nov. 29, 2015.

130. ^ Rhode Island is the only U.S. state with a Dutch name. Adriaan Block from Amsterdam sailed past it in 1614 and was impressed by the red color of the clay. Believing he was looking at an island, he named it Roode Eylandt, red island. Today's name is a corruption of that.

131. ^ *Patients at Hasbro Children's Hospital get a special "Good Night Lights" display*, ABC6 News, Dec. 28, 2020.

132. ^ Alexandra Zaslow, *Entire town secretly learns sign language to give a deaf man best day of his life*, People Magazine, March 11, 2015.

133. ^ Alexander Hamilton, June 18, 1787, Records of the Federal Convention.

134. ^ Letter from Henry Knox to Rufus King, June 8, 1787.

135. ^ Letter from Theodore Sedgwick to Nathan Dane, July 5, 1787.

136. ^ Frances Folsom Cleveland's youngest granddaughter, Margaret Folsom Cleveland, born 92 years after her grandmother, spent most of her life in and around Portland,

Maine. She was a driving force behind Portland's YWCA, empowering women when and wherever she could. Margaret passed away in Scarborough, in 2021.

137. ^ King, pp 77-78.

138. ^ Bruce Watson, *Frances Perkins Brought You the Weekend*, American Heritage, Spring edition 2021.

139. ^ Max Richtman, *Honoring Frances Perkins, the 'Mother' of Social Security*, March 26, 2019.

140. ^ Reader's Digest, July 2013. By early 2023, there were over 150,000 little free libraries all over the world.

141. ^ Candice Millard, *Destiny of the Republic, A Tale of Madness, Medicine and the Murder of a President*, pp 206-207.

142. ^ Gavin Weightman, *The Frozen Ice Trade*, p211.

143. ^ Andrew Barton, Alan White and Charles Cogbill, *Reconstructing the Past: Maine Forests Then and Now*, Northern Woodlands, July 3, 2013.

144. ^ Report of the Chief of Engineers U.S. Army 1911, p1163.

145. ^ Weightman, p223.

146. ^ Thomas Hobbes wrote *Leviathan* in 1651. In it, he advocated a system of iron-fisted government, for without firm leadership, he said, people would make a mess of things. Each day would then be filled with *"worst of all, continual fear, and danger of violent death; and the life of man, solitary, poor, nasty, brutish, and short."*

147. ^ Jean Jacques Rousseau summed up this sentiment in his autobiography *Confessions*.

148. ^ Matthew 6:34.

149. ^ The Fuerza Aérea Uruguaya plane that flew into an Andes mountainside on October 13, 1972 was a Fokker Fairchild that carried five crew members and forty members of a rugby team. Sixteen people survived the crash. They kept themselves alive for two months by eating the flesh of deceased fellow passengers. They were rescued by helicopters just before Christmas that year.

150. ^ Ecclesiastes 1-2.

151. ^ Eleanor Porter, *Pollyanna: The First Glad Book*. It was followed by a volume two, *Pollyanna Grows Up: The Second Glad Book*. Six other writers published another twelve sequels over the years.

152. ^ Peter Bernstein, *The Power of Gold, The History of an Obsession*, p20.

153. ^ Exodus 25-28.

154. ^ John Ruskin, *The King of the Golden River*, p62.

155. ^ Genesis 2:11.

156. ^ Data from Maine Department of Agriculture, Conservation & Forestry.

157. ^ Timothy Green, *The World of Gold*, pp405-407.

158. ^ Peter Millard and Stephan Kueffner, *The Sinking Gold Town*, Bloomberg, July 22, 2022.

159. ^ Katrien Meert, Mario Pandelaere, Vanessa Patrick, *Taking a shine to it: How the preference for glossy stems from an innate need for water*, Dec 27, 2013, also: Journal of Consumer Psychology, volume 24, pp195-206, April 2014.

160. ^ Nehemiah 6:8.

161. ^ Thomas Jefferson, *A Summary View of the Rights of British America*, 1774.

162. ^ Earl Warren was called as a witness before the U.S. House Select Committee Investigating National Defense Migration. He testified Feb. 28, 1942 in his capacity as California's state Attorney General.

163. ^ In his memoir published three years after his death in 1974, Warren expressed regret about his call for locking up Japanese Americans. *"When I thought of the innocent little children who were torn from home, school friends, and congenial surroundings, I was conscience-stricken."*

164. ^ The Wheeling, West Virginia Intelligencer, Feb. 10, 1950.

165. ^ Sermon, May 9, 1798.

166. ^ The Alien Act of 1798 temporarily gave the U.S. president the right to have non-residents arrested and/or kicked out of the country. Freedom of speech was restricted regarding calling for secession from the new republic. Four years later, the law was repealed.

167. ^ Robert Goldberg, *Enemies Within, The Culture of Conspiracy in Modern America*, p49.

168. ^ Jennifer Hecht, *Doubt, A History*, p442.

169. ^ Jennifer Finney Boylan, *It's Not Easy Being an Optimist in Maine*, New York Times, Oct. 14, 2020.

170. ^ Hecht, p492.

171. ^ Erik Shilling, *Meet the Professor Behind the First Printed Use of Shit Happens*, Atlas Obscura, Feb 26, 2016.

172. ^ They were not the most reliable media: the first was *National Spotlite*, whose reporter claimed to have slipped into a storage room inside Disney's hospital where he found Disney in a cylinder. The story was picked up by *Ici Paris*, *The National Tattler* and *Midnight*, the latter with the headline *Walt Disney Is Being Kept Alive in Deep Freeze*. Neal Gabler, *Walt Disney, The Triumph of the American Imagination*, p8.

173. ^ Hannah Farber, *Underwriters of the United States, How Insurance Shaped the American Founding*, p243.

174. ^ Ibid. p61.

175. ^ The Wright brothers were descendants of Dutchman Cornelius van Cleef through their dad's grandmother Margaret van Cleve. The brothers were bicycle makers. They marketed their best-selling bicycle as the Van Cleve.

176. ^ Robert Malthus, *An Essay on the Principle of Population*, 1798.

177. ^ Mauro Guillén, p11.

178. ^ Beth Waterhouse, *A Sustainable Future*, PBS-TV.

179. ^ National Geographic, *Netherlands Feeds the World*, September 2017.

180. ^ Joe Hasell and Max Roser, *Famines*, Our World in Data, Oxford University, Dec. 7, 2017.

181. ^ Alex de Waal, *The end of famine? Prospects for the elimination of mass starvation by political action*, Political Geography, Elsevier, p184.

182. ^ By the U.S. Department of Agriculture's definition, a farm is any place where $1000 or more worth of agricultural products are produced and sold in the course of a year, or would normally have been sold.

183. ^ Mira Katbamna, *Half a good man is better than none at all*, The Guardian Oct 26, 2009, also: Kate Bolick, *All the single ladies*, The Atlantic, November 2011.

184. ^ Tim Marshall, *Prisoners of Geography*, p40.

185. ^ Mauro Guillén, p20.

186. ^ Martin King White, Wang Feng, Yong Cai, *Challenging Myths About China's One-Child Policy*, China Journal 74, p144-159.

187. ^ Amartya Sen, *Women's Progress Outdid China's One-Child Policy*, New York Times, Nov 2, 2015.

188. ^ Rachel Nuwer, *Singapore's "National Night" Encourages Citizens to Make Babies*, Smithsonian Magazine, Aug. 8, 2012.

189. ^ *The Great Human Odyssey*, CBC Canada.

190. ^ Elizabeth Fenn, *Pox Americana, The Great Smallpox Epidemic of 1775-82*, p5.

191. ^ *Fortune Smiles on Unluckiest Man*, The Scotsman, June 18, 2003.

192. ^ Mark Kruger, *Why Are the Chinese People So Optimistic?* Yicai Global, Feb 21, 2022.

193. ^ Stepan Goncharov, *Who is Optimistic About the Future of Russia - And Why?*, Riddle, Kennan Institute, Apr 18, 2018.

194. ^ The Rocket eBook was bought by Gemstar-TV Guide, a company now owned by Robert Murdoch's News Corp. It

never achieved a serious market share once Amazon and the Barnes and Noble bookstore chain simultaneously moved into selling e-books. By Christmas 2009, during that year's holiday sales, the competition between Amazon's Kindle and B&N's Nook dominated the market. Amazon eventually emerged as the big winner. The Nook has since disappeared from the market altogether.

195. ^ Guillén, p12.

196. ^ United Nations Migration Report, 2015.

197. ^ Harry McGee, *How the Mobile Phone Changed Kenya*, Irish Times, May 14, 2016.

198. ^ Njoroge, Zurovac, Ogara, Chuma and Kirigia, *Assessing the Feasibility of Ehealth and Mhealth: a Systematic Review and Analysis of Initiatives Implemented in Kenya*, BMC Research Notes 10, pp90-101.

199. ^ Mauro Guillén, very first sentence in *2030*, pVII.

200. ^ Ray Mwareya: *A South African City Says It's Putting QR Codes On Informal Settlement Cabins To Help Services. But Residents And Privacy Experts Are Uncertain*, Buzzfeed, Aug 15, 2022.

201. ^ Emiko Terazono, *African farming: cassava now the center of attention*, Financial Times Jan 21, 2014.

202. ^ Nicole Svajlenka, *Immigrant Workers Are Important to Filling Growing Occupations*, Center for American Progress, 11 May 2017.

203. ^ Anupam Jena, *US Immigration Policiy and American Medical Research, Annals of Internal Medicine 167*, pp584-586.

204. ^ Reagan's doctors and nurses had names like Morales, Giordano, Lichtmann, May Chin and Sidou. They came from Nicaragua, Mexico, Guatemala, Malaysia, Germany and Greece.

205. ^ Washington Post, June 28, 2013.

206. ^ United Nations Migration Report 2015, also: *Is Migration Good for the Economy*, OECD 2014, also: Giovanni Peri, *Immigration, Productivity and Labor Markets*, Journal of Economic Perspectives 30, pp3-30, also: David Autor, *Why Are There Still So Many Jobs*, Journal of Economic Perspectives 29, pp3-30.

207. ^ Data from US Census 2020.

208. ^ In 2022, the U.S. had 75 million residents aged sixty and older. The number of Millennials was 72 million, a huge number for one generation born between 1981 and 1996.

209. ^ Edward Bok, *The Mother of America*, The Ladies Home Journal, October 1903, p16. "For years we have written in our histories and taught in our schools that this nation is a transplanted England," wrote Bok, editor of the Journal, before adding that America's mother "came directly from Holland."

210. ^ In *The Dutch Touch* (Balans, Amsterdam, 2019), my book about the abundant Dutch fingerprints on America's present-day landscape, I list the locations of the cradles that once rocked the Roosevelts (Tholen, the Netherlands), the Rockefellers (Breskens), the Vanderbilts (De Bilt), the Fonda's (Kollum), the Brando's (Utrecht), the DeNiro's (Monnickendam), the Cronkites (Naarden), and many other American names that most people would not immediately associate with their Dutch ancestry.

211. ^ The military leader of Holland's Seven Provinces was Prince Maurice of Orange-Nassau, the political leader was Prime Minister Johan van Oldenbarnevelt, and the ideologue was philosopher Hugo Grotius. He escaped from life imprisonment inside a moat-surrounded castle by hiding in a book chest that was carried out by his captors. Today his image hangs in the U.S. House of Representatives, to the right of the Speaker's podium. America

is honoring Grotius for his contribution to international maritime law.

212. ^ Marshall, p58.

213. ^ David Frum, *China Is a Paper Dragon*, The Atlantic, May 3, 2021, also: Michael Beckley, *Unrivaled: Why America Will Remain the World's Sole Superpower.*

214. ^ Mark Kurlansky: *Paper, Paging Through History*, p. 224. To date twenty-six copies of the Declaration of Independence have been found, as well as Jefferson's first draft. The paper sheets came from three different Dutch papermakers, Lubbertus Van Gerrevink who had his own papermaking windmill in the coastal town of Egmond, the Honig family, and Dirk and Cornelius Blauw, all three from Zaandam, just north of Amsterdam.

215. ^ The USS Maine had a large cargo of ammunition on board, and on the night of February 15, 1898, it exploded in the ship's forward holds. Of the 355 crew members, only 16 were unharmed. The death toll was 261. Spain did not sink the Maine. The explosion was caused by self-ignition in one of the ship's coal bunkers. In 1976, Admiral Hyman Rickover concluded after what to date is the most thorough investigation of the ship's demise, "There is no evidence that the Maine was destroyed by a mine."

216. ^ The instrument of impeachment was a Benjamin Franklin idea. As ambassador to Paris, he had watched with surprise how in the Netherlands Stadholder Prince William V had sabotaged his own government's decision to merge the Dutch fleet with France's in order to stand up together against England, and thereby to support the new American republic. This should never happen in America, Franklin insisted, where all powers that be ought to be held accountable. He won the argument, and America has had impeachment proceedings since 1789.

217. ^ Erin Brown, *Money flows into fertility technology*, Axios, Jan. 25, 2023.

218. ^ The general US fertility rate in 2021 was 56.6 births per 1,000 women ages 15–44, up one percent from 2020. *Births Rose for the First Time in Seven Years in 2021*, CDC, National Center for Health Statistics, May 24, 2022, also: Martha J. Bailey, Janet Currie, and Hannes Schwandt, *The Covid-19 Baby Bump: The Unexpected Increase in U.S. Fertility Rates in Response to the Pandemic*, National Bureau of Economic Research, Oct 2022.

219. ^ Erik Schatzker, *Hertz Order for 100,000 EVs Sends Tesla Value to $1 Trillion*, Bloomberg, Oct 25, 2021, also: David Welch and Rick Clough, *Hertz Plans to Buy 175,000 Electric Vehicles From GM Over Five Years*, Bloomberg Sept 20, 2022.

220. ^ *Survey: Job Engagement Declines For A Third of Workers; Remote Work Is Not to Blame*, The Conference Board, Oct 18, 2022, also: *Societal Leadership Is Now a Core Function of Business*, 2022 Edelman Trust Barometer, Sept. 2, 2022.

221. ^ *France: The Helicopter Caper*, Time Magazine, June 9, 1986.

222. ^ Adam Azra'el, *The Vaujour Escape*, thelesserstories.com.

223. ^ Matthew 25:36.

224. ^ Daniel Michaels and Marina Rozenman, *These Days, French Prisoners Find Walls Not So Daunting*, Wall Street Journal, Aug. 29, 2002.

225. ^ John Voelcker, *1.2 Billion Vehicles on Roads Worldwide Now, 2 Billion in 2035*, greencarreports.com, July 29, 2014.

226. ^ *Maryland, Fatal Copter Crash*, New York Times, July 24, 2009.

227. ^ *Maryland Helicopter Crash Ruled Accidental*, Washington Post, July 30, 2010.

www.ingramcontent.com/pod-product-compliance
Lightning Source LLC
Chambersburg PA
CBHW060907140726
47996CB00001B/157